THE LAST DAYS OF THE
STEAM
RAILWAY

THE LAST DAYS OF THE
STEAM
RAILWAY

EDITED BY

ALAN POSTLETHWAITE

SUTTON PUBLISHING

First published in the United Kingdom in 1997 by
Sutton Publishing Limited · Phoenix Mill
Thrupp · Stroud · Gloucestershire · GL5 2BU

British Library Cataloguing in Publication Data
A catalogue record for this book is available from the British Library

ISBN 0-7509-1504-8

Endpapers: front: Class A4 Pacific No. 60029 *Woodcock* is a fine sight, emerging from Stoke Tunnel with the Up 'Norseman' – the 12.10 Newcastle Tyne Commission Quay to King's Cross (*Hugh Ballantyne*); back: Fowler 0–6–0 class 4F No. 44182 brings a mineral train off the spur from the Midland line at Stamford onto Great Northern metals alongside the passenger and goods stations of Stamford Town. (*Alan Postlethwaite*)

Half-title: LNER class A4 Pacific *Commonwealth of Australia* at the head of the Down 'Flying Scotsman' at Newcastle Central. It was one of five locomotives built in 1937 for 'The Coronation' six-hour schedule between London and Edinburgh. Its livery was restored in August 1947 to 'garter blue' after the wartime years in unlined black. 'Coronation' locomotives always had stainless steel lettering and numbers but following restoration, the original LNER No. 4491 was replaced by No. 12.

(*Kenneth Oldham, April 1948*)

Half-title verso: 'There be none of Riddles' daughters with a fleetness like thee; and with fourteen cars a-hauling, show thy vaporosity!' This adaptation of a Lord Byron poem is a tribute to the 'Britannia' class Pacifics of which 55 were built at Crewe between 1951 and 1954. This is No. 70031 *Byron* on the LMS main line between Stafford and Colwich, where electrification posts have recently appeared. The 'Britannias' performed well during their short lives. What a pity that none was named after Sir John Betjeman, poet and occasional writer on railways. He became laureate too late, alas.

(*Alan Postlethwaite, 21.7.62*)

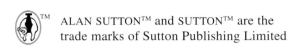 ALAN SUTTON™ and SUTTON™ are the trade marks of Sutton Publishing Limited

Typeset in 12/17pt Sabon.
Typesetting and origination by
Sutton Publishing Limited.
Printed in Great Britain by
Butler & Tanner, Frome, Somerset.

CONTENTS

A mineral train comes off the spur from the Midland line at Stamford onto Great Northern metals alongside the passenger and goods stations of Stamford Town. It is signalled to bear right to cross the Midland line and to junction with the LNWR at Wansford (headquarters of the preserved Nene Valley Railway). The Fowler 0–6–0 class 4F No. 44182 represents a class of 772 locomotives which were introduced by the Midland Railway in 1911. Note the tall semaphore signal gantry.

(Alan Postlethwaite, 20.3.63)

Introduction – The Magic of an Old Institution

Railways were an integral part of the Industrial Revolution, together with coal-mining, mass production of iron and steel, manufacturing and almost universal use of steam power. The steam locomotive was developed gradually for over a century, reaching a zenith in the mid-twentieth century. Carriages and wagons were likewise improved gradually, continuing to this day. The railway infrastructure, on the other hand, was subject to less continual improvement. There were important changes, of course, such as in track design, gauge standardization, urban electrification and the rationalization of major stations and yards. For the most part, however, the cuttings, embankments, bridges, signals, stations, services and staffing structure remained essentially as established in the mid- to late nineteenth century, although with various accumulations of vegetation, soot and tradition. To the general public, the railways were a social institution, as solid a rock as Parliament itself, a familiar and dependable part of everyday life, blending with landscape and townscape. They had existed for as long as anyone could remember and were regarded as irreplaceable – expected to last forever, more or less in the same form but with further improvements in rolling stock. Well into nationalization, the nation depended upon and loved its steam railways.

During the late 1950s and 1960s, a series of bold political, technical and social changes were implemented which quickly extinguished the steam railway, closed a third of the route mileage and dropped much of the freight traffic. Forces that contributed to these changes were the Railway Modernization Plan, the rise of personal wealth and car ownership, government commitment to road development and a new British Railways Board committed to economic viability, whose first chairman was a no-nonsense businessman from ICI, Dr Richard Beeching. By the 1970s, the nation had entered a new age of progress which depended less upon the railway and had no place for steam.

Other facets of change during the postwar years were improved educational opportunities, shorter working hours and new, affordable photographic technologies in the shops. A small army of railway enthusiasts evolved to take advantage of these changes, travelling widely and photographing the steam railway. Line closures and 'very last days' of steam naturally attracted enthusiasts by the train-load, but it was the individual photographer who captured the true character of the railway by recording a multitude of ordinary scenes and activities, without the distractions of special events. Those who started in the 1950s, unaware of the cataclysmic changes ahead, took photographs at leisure and with a certain innocence and abandon, but as the 1960s progressed there was increased panic to record as many lines and services as possible. This book is a tribute to all the photographers who recorded for posterity both the ordinary and special scenes during the reign of steam on British Railways (BR) and the Ulster Transport Authority (UTA).

So what did they photograph? Certainly the locomotives – ranging from BR standard designs, through the interwar years of the Big Four (LMS, LNER, GWR and SR), to the remnants of a hundred or so pre-Group companies of the late nineteenth and early twentieth centuries. The variety of locomotives seemed infinite – one was continually surprised by what turned up and by the contrasts between old and new. These surprises were made all the sweeter by the variety of carriages and wagons which also stretched back to pre-Group days. Although colour and cleanliness were in decline, distinctive design features shone through and captured the imagination. An express train might transport the mind's eye to the 'modern' age of the 1930s when world records were being shattered in all modes of transport. Similarly, a branch train could take one back to the age of Edwardian elegance, just prior to the First World War, when Europe had such freedom and opportunity. The older steam trains were therefore time machines, which accounted for much of their fascination. The new 'standard' designs of BR were admirable and well photographed, but they were not regarded at the time with the same reverence. Looking back now, of course, the BR designs have grown almost to match their predecessors in historical interest and significance.

After the chance to capture the locomotives, especially old ones, what else did the steam railway offer the intrepid photographer? Next in line was the infrastructure: the whole gamut of station paraphernalia – sheds, yards and pointwork, boxes and signals, the backs of houses and industries, great bridges, viaducts and tunnels, and miles of cuttings, embankments and telegraph lines through pastures, woods and moorland to connect with the next junction or town. Any of these could be photographed individually, but they only came to life when combined with steam, smoke and the sense of movement provided by a locomotive, especially at the head of an interesting train. Keen railway photographers therefore sought the best settings of town and countryside in which to depict the train, and composition became as important as the train itself. The photographer was both archivist and artist.

The final topic of photography was people. The steam railway was overflowing with railwaymen, a legacy of the age of cheap labour, now coming to an end. Not only did governments offer the prospect of progress and personal wealth, the trades unions demanded it! And so it happened, but at the cost of job losses in the name of productivity and economy. Porters, shunters and firemen became virtually extinct, and the numbers of drivers, signalmen, fitters, trackmen, guards, ticket clerks, managers, etc. were drastically reduced as a result of new technologies, modern management practices and the shrinking of the railway system. Third- and fourth-generation railwaymen came to the end of their line, no longer wanted, while those who remained had to learn new practices in a new working environment. Tradition and camaraderie were in decline and the railway was becoming a less familiar and less friendly institution. Passengers too were part of the social scene and are of particular interest for their clothing – fashions can often date a picture just as readily as trains and advertisements. Pictures of steam railway people are part of social history, recording a way of life on its way out. We are therefore indebted to those photographers who took the trouble to record the railway people, both in portrait and as part of a wider railway scene.

The chapters in this book are devoted to various aspects of the steam railway as seen through the lens of the enthusiast-photographer. He would visit hundreds of stations and walk hundreds of track-miles to compile a collection of pictures which would capture the atmosphere of an area. He was always on the look-out for that special location and composition which would take his breath away. Steam had a magic quality, some call it romance, that could excite the heart and mind of both the casual traveller and the knowledgeable enthusiast. The magic was infused through a combination of senses, usually starting with sound – a signal bell, a level-crossing gate crashing open, an exhaust beat, a whistle or safety valve blowing, the swish of air being penetrated at speed, the rumble of steel upon steel and the clackety-clack over the rail-breaks. The magic was heightened by the spectacle of a violent exhaust-mix of steam and smoke which lingered on the breeze. Then a colourful train was seen to be propelled by an intricate side-mechanism which rotated, rocked and reciprocated at a frightening speed, too fast for the eye. One might also glimpse the engine crew at work, hand on brake or stoking the fire, with a glow of orange-yellow fire flooding the cab at night. Immediately after its passing came the smell – an unholy mix of sulphurous smoke laced with steam, often accompanied by the fall-out of sooty grit and water droplets which splattered one's clothes and entered any open window, especially near the front of the train – the days of steam were not clean. As the train disappeared, the dust, leaves and litter would re-settle and silence would return, more noticeable now after such an uproar. One stood still for a moment, appreciating the event and waiting for the mind to resume its equilibrium.

In stations and yards, one could witness a similar magic but in slow motion, with the added smells of hot lubricating oil, grease and ash, and with time to study the aesthetics of the locomotive – a long boiler bristling with attachments, a shapely chimney and smokebox, the intricate wheels, brakes, cylinders and associated mechanisms, the line of the buffer-beam and frame, the firebox and cab design, water-tanks or a tender, and the great bunker bristling with coaling tools. Looking into the cab, one could discover the polished controls and indicators, with crewmen who were always congenial, having been 'touched' by that same magic which has been passed on to the likes of us, so many years on! To meet the crew was to want to ride with them, to train as a fireman and driver, to work long hours in all weathers for meagre wages – in short, to immerse oneself in the romance of steam.

Film writers and producers made good use of the steam railway as a setting for thrillers and romances. Who could ever forget the passion of Noel Coward's *Brief Encounter*, much of which was set at night in the Victorian buffet and on the platforms of Carnforth station? The blossoming love affair is interrupted skilfully by the ringing of platform bells and the passing of Anglo-Scottish expresses at speed, while human partings, contemplations and regrets are enacted on the local train, headed by a clanking Stanier 2–6–4 tank No. 2429, to the strains of Rachmaninov's Piano Concerto No. 2. Another great heart-wrencher was *The Railway Children*, set upon a delightful country branch line. Then there were the thrillers made by the likes of Ealing Studios, ending with a police chase through marshalling yards, with the villain coming to a nasty end with a rolling wagon. By contrast, Alfred Hitchcock used open lines in Scotland as settings for the spy drama, *The Thirty-Nine Steps*. What they all drew upon was the romance and fascination of steam railways, to enhance the story, and to suggest a sense of escape to far-off places. That too is what the enthusiast craves – the opportunity to jump onto any train to distant locations. He does so regularly in his mind and occasionally 'for real'.

To summarize, the magic and fascination of steam railways stem from three considerations – of the past, the present and the future. What was it like when this train was built? What a glorious spectacle this train makes! What would it be like to travel to this train's destination? As you contemplate the pictures herein, pause to consider which of these feelings dominates. If you can sense all three in one picture, then the photographer has done an excellent job.

Not all steam enthusiasts were brilliant photographers, of course. Some were opportunist snapshot takers, while others did not bother with the camera at all. The non-photographers include the great travellers, timetable experts, sound-recordists, writers, historians, modellers, locomotive performance buffs, collectors of engine numbers, tickets or railway memorabilia, and that most noble band of all, the preservationists, who commit their spare time almost exclusively to fund-raising, restoration, promotion and operation of particular lines and rolling stock. They are 'noble' because they forego the luxury of idle leisure to endure the hard work of implementing projects. If the photographer is the artist, archivist and purveyor of dreams, the preservationist is the worker, manager and marketeer of reality – he learns the harsh business of running a real railway. Everyone thinks he knows how to run a railway, and we are often quick to condemn when something goes wrong, but to do it 'for real' requires skill, hard work and the greatness to live with mistakes. Running a railway harnesses the resources of people, materials, assets and money to achieve company goals in both the short and the long term. The large number of preserved railways and rolling stock in service today bears testimony to the achievements of this 'aristocracy' of enthusiasts, and a chapter of this book is devoted to their early achievements, using pictures of locomotives and lines that were subsequently preserved. Thanks to them, today's children can still enjoy the magic of steam.

The pictures have been chosen for their technical quality, artistic merit and railway interest. There are five chapters depicting different types of train plus specialist chapters on locomotives, people and preservation. Each chapter provides contrasts between the Big Four, BR, the UTA and remnants of the pre-Group era – the variety is at times staggering. Nine photographers have contributed, providing further contrasts in style, from technically flawless pictures of engines to highly 'atmospheric' portraits in smoky locations, and great landscapes on remote fells. As you contemplate the achievements of the locomotive builders and railway companies, pause for a moment to consider also the trouble that the photographers took to produce these pictures – the planning, travelling, tramping of lines, waiting, recording of details, processing, storing, cataloguing and writing up. The photographers were young at the time, generally with limited resources of time and money. Nearly all the pictures are published here for the first time – indeed, many have never before been printed, having lain dormant for decades in dark cupboards and lofts.

Finally, spare a thought for those who built the railways, from the armies of rugged navvies who toiled, lived and often died on the lines, to the directors and engineers who instigated and designed them and made all the key decisions. Although it is seldom brought out in photographs and captions, railways are built and run just as much from the office as from the track and workshop. A sad reminder is when the Allied POWs who built the Burma Railway had to concede in the end that it was not so much their achievement as that of the Japanese. Indeed, many would argue that direction from a central office is more fundamental than heaving a shovel or fitting a piston. So let us celebrate the achievements of all grades of railwayman – manual, technical, clerical and managerial – when looking at the pictures. It was their team effort that brought us the enduring magic of steam.

MAIN LINES AND LONG-DISTANCE EXPRESSES

At Euston, LMS 'Jubilee' class 4–6–0 No. 45684 *Jutland* simmers gently in platform 2. In *The Great British Railway Station Euston* (Irwell Press, 1994), this platform is described by Ellaway as 'a beautiful place where light poured in from the right and the station shrank into darkness . . . to the left'. The date is between 1957 (tender emblem) and December 1960 when 45684 was transferred from Crewe North to Willesden.

(H.G. Usmar/David Hucknall collection)

Our journey begins on the main lines, known also as trunk routes – what we would nowadays call the Intercity network. They are characterized by long, modern trains running on fast, multiple tracks between city stations of great size, prestige and architectural merit. One thinks immediately of the famous termini in London, Glasgow and Liverpool, as well as great through-stations and junctions at Edinburgh, York, Birmingham, Cardiff and Bristol among others. The major through-stations were full of surprises for the traveller, with trains arriving from unexpected directions and the hustle and bustle of passengers, parcels and luggage, culminating with the slamming of doors, guards' whistles and the distant sound of a steam engine getting under way. By contrast, departure from a terminus was more civilized, with clean carriages, time to find one's seat and the opportunity to inspect the engine. Terminal arrivals were also sedate, with a last chance to view the engine and a sense of achievement for the crew and for the railway as a whole – one thinks of all the preparation, furnace-stoking, signal-pulling and services that contributed to that single journey.

Long journeys by steam were generally in compartments where a 'club atmosphere' would prevail. The fatigue of travel was made pleasurable by light conversation with fellow inmates, by occasional escapes along the corridor and by visiting the buffet car or restaurant car. One of the most pleasurable experiences on trains is a full lunch or dinner, especially if accompanied by good wine, good company and fine scenery to admire through the window. One memorable experience was to take lunch through the Peak District in an LMS dining car when it was snowing, enjoying the contrast between the warm, friendly, sumptuous interior and the cold, threatening barrenness outside. A similar cosiness was achieved in Griddle cars travelling to exposed outposts like the Kyle of Lochalsh. The comforts of the dining car protected the traveller from the harsh conditions without.

The scenery from express trains can vary from hour to hour, from suburban beginnings, through a patchwork of farmland with animals and crops, along a coastline or river perhaps, and then over the great moorlands with their scenery of towering uplands. The rural scene is broken periodically by country stations, towns and junctions whose complex pointwork interrupts the natural rhythm of the rail-joints. Some expresses were truly non-stop – King's Cross to Newcastle, Paddington to Cardiff, for example – and these provided a great sense of exclusive achievement for both the crew and passengers. Other trains stopped at one or more intermediate stations, generally great places which were full of activity but spoiling that sense of achievement which now had to be shared with others. A feature guaranteed to breathe new life into the dozing traveller was the tunnel, especially a long one, for one knew instinctively that the scenery at the far end would be different, like entering new world.

The pleasure of long-distance travel was enhanced by the naming of crack expresses. A further touch of romance was the naming of steam engines, the origins and logic of which could be quite obscure. In this chapter alone, we find engines named after a poet, a duchess, a game bird, a racehorse, a sea battle, a regiment, part of a golf course, two cities, a county, a couple of castles, a dominion, a royal event, an engine designer and a railway manager who bore an uncanny resemblance to 'Useless Eustace' in the *Daily Mirror* (an unjust caricature if it was intentional, since Sir Eustace rose to eminence from quite humble beginnings as a railway clerk). In *The Beauty of Old Trains* (George Allen and Unwin, 1952), C. Hamilton Ellis describes the art of engine naming as 'a pleasing and civilised practice, adding just that leaven of fancy to existing fact that lifts our mechanical civilisation out of the rationalist rut. . . . It adds not a ha'porth of difference to the efficient working of a railway, and therein lies part of its charm.'

The locomotives in this first chapter are predominantly LNER and LMS, the companies that competed during the interwar years for world records. The scheduled non-stop distance records achieved during 1927–8 were successively Euston to Carnforth (236 miles), King's Cross to Newcastle (268 miles), Euston to Carlisle (300 miles), and King's Cross to Edinburgh (393 miles). The LMS had the last word, however, by virtue of its longer distance up the West Coast from Euston, achieving 400 miles to Edinburgh and 401 miles to Glasgow.

World speed records for steam were set in 1935 by the LNER with class A4 Pacifics *Papyrus* (108 m.p.h.) and *Silver Link* (112 m.p.h.). In 1937, the LMS achieved 114 m.p.h. with *Coronation*, but the world record which stands to this day was set in 1938 by the LNER with *Mallard* at 126 m.p.h.

Wallow awhile in the beauty of the express trains which follow. Look at their length and composition, the variety of coaches and vans. Feel the power and energy of the locomotive suggested by steam issuing from the exhaust, cylinders and safety valves. Examine the length of the great boilers, their casings and attachments. Admire the wheels, cylinders and 'motion' – mostly Pacifics plus a few 4–6–0s and a lone tank engine from Belfast. Compare the designs of the Big Four and of BR and pay homage to those designers who took the trouble to add that little extra to create a machine of genuine beauty. In the expresses, you are looking at the zenith of British steam design.

An immaculate Peppercorn class A1 Pacific No. 60119 awaits departure from King's Cross with the 'Queen of Scots' Pullman express. Built in November 1948, this locomotive was not named *Patrick Sterling* until July 1950. There were fifty in the class; it was one of the few classes of Pacific to be built after the Second World War. None is preserved, but a new one is currently under construction.

(Kenneth Oldham, April 1950)

On the East Coast main line south of Grantham, class V2 No. 60872 *King's Own Yorkshire Light Infantry* passes High Dyke on the approach to Stoke Tunnel with the 9.14 a.m. from York to King's Cross. This 2–6–2 class was introduced by Sir Nigel Gresley in 1936. Originally intended for the 'Green Arrow' fast freight service to Scotland, it became a versatile mixed traffic class. Of the 184 built, only 8 carried a name. In the sidings, trains of loaded iron ore tipplers are ready for despatch the following Monday to the Scunthorpe area.

(Hugh Ballantyne, 19.8.61)

Emerging from under Bathwick Hill on the approach to Bath Spa, the 12.30 p.m. Paddington to Weston-super-Mare is headed by a rare tandem of Great Western 4–6–0s of mixed generations and character. The pilot is No. 1019 *County of Merioneth* of F.W. Hawksworth's 'County' class which was introduced in 1945. The train engine is No. 5027 *Farleigh Castle* of C.B. Collett's 'Castle' class, introduced in 1923. The former, designed for fast, mixed traffic, has smaller wheels and a higher boiler pressure than the pre-war passenger express class.

(Hugh Ballantyne, 12.7.59)

A stalwart of St Margaret's depot in Edinburgh was LNER class A1 Pacific No. 60152 *Holyrood*; it was seen regularly working both passenger and freight traffic over the 'Waverley Route' to Carlisle and also into Newcastle up the East Coast main line. Here she is preparing to depart with a train for Berwick-on-Tweed (right), while 4–6–0 class B1 No. 61147 (left) fills Waverley station with an unholy mix of smoke and steam, moving slowly from beneath the canopy at the head of empty coaching stock, bound for Craigentinny sidings.

(Brian J. Dickson, 21.3.64)

LMS Pacific No. 46225 *Duchess of Gloucester* brings an Up express past the LNWR signal-box at Winwick Junction onto a quadruple section of the West Coast main line (just north of Warrington). The line to the left leads to Earlstown Junction for both Liverpool and Manchester. This was part of the Grand Junction Railway which amalgamated in 1845 with the Liverpool &

Manchester and London & Birmingham railways to become the London & North Western Railway – the 'Premier Line'. The factory beyond is the Vulcan Foundry, makers of steam locomotives from 1830 until 1956.

(Hugh Ballantyne, 29.8.63)

After the austerity of the immediate postwar years, LNER class A3 Pacific No. 60092 *Fairway* is a splendid sight in immaculate apple-green livery as it thunders through Retford with a Newcastle to London express. The BR number and full title are displayed on the cab sides and tender of this Heaton-based locomotive, but the buffer-beam number has been replaced by a standard BR plate on the smokebox door. An old six-wheeled passenger brake stands in the adjacent siding.

(Kenneth Oldham, 8.4.50)

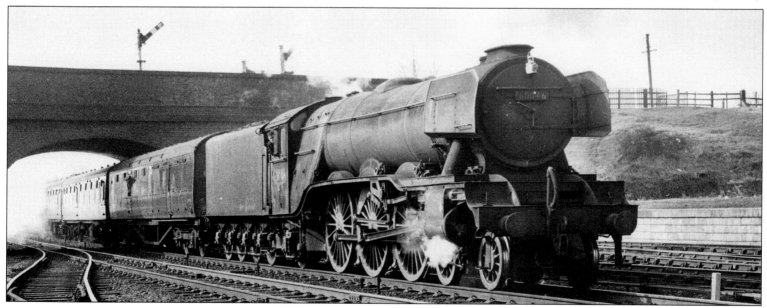

Two months before its withdrawal, a grimy A3 Pacific No. 60046 *Diamond Jubilee* heads a Sunday morning service from King's Cross to Peterborough on the East Coast main line at Huntingdon. This class was a development of the original Gresley Pacific, introduced by the Great Northern Railway in 1922. A total of seventy-eight were built for express passenger duty. It was a most handsome design, characterized by the upswept running plate, prominent steam pipes and the blending of the firebox casing with the circumference of the huge boiler. The German-style smoke deflectors were a late addition.

(Eric Sawford, 7.4.63)

At Plymouth North Road, two Great Western 4–6–0s exude violent columns of smoke and steam. Heading for Penzance, No. 7006 *Lydford Castle* (right) restarts and will take the Cornwall loop (right) towards the Royal Albert Bridge. The line to the left leads to the Great Western Docks, the former Ocean Terminal and the former terminus of Millbay. North Road was built as a joint station, with GWR and LSWR trains from Exeter arriving from opposite directions. The LSWR terminus at Plymouth Friary was on the other side of town.

(Alan Postlethwaite, 5.9.59)

Although built to the Irish standard gauge of 5 ft 3 in, the class WT 2–6–4 tank has a design pedigree which clearly belongs to the LMS (see pp. 26, 40). Eighteen were built at Derby between 1947 and 1950 and one is preserved at Whitehead, Co. Antrim. Looking clean and smart in its black livery, lined in red and yellow, No. 53 heads the 12.30 p.m. express from Great Victoria Street, Belfast to Amiens Street, Dublin (now called Connolly). Photographed at Portadown, the locomotive will work as far as Dundalk where a CIE diesel will take over.

(Hugh Ballantyne, 31.8.64)

One of the last days of main line steam in Northern Ireland. Seated on the right of the cab with hand on brake and watching the line ahead, the driver of the 2.45 p.m. from Dublin brings his train down the 1 in 100 Wellington Bank towards Goraghwood, some 42 miles from Belfast. Class WT 2–6–4 tank No. 53 was a locomotive of the Northern Counties Committee, here running on the Great Northern main line.

(Hugh Ballantyne, 31.8.64)

Opposite: A stranger in paradise, Great Western 4–6–0 No. 7029 *Clun Castle* crosses the King Edward VII bridge over the Tyne to or from Gateshead depot. The engine was undergoing clearance tests on the East Coast main line between York and Newcastle, in preparation for its use on excursions the following month. It was stabled at Gateshead before moving south for further tests. According to contemporary journals, it just cleared the edges of Newcastle's platform 9 but failed to negotiate the others.

(David Hucknall, 19.8.67)

The principal summits on the West Coast main line are at Shap (915 ft), Beattock (1,015 ft) and, for Edinburgh trains only, Cobbinshaw (880 ft). Beattock station was surprisingly large, with extensive sidings and an engine shed. LMS Pacific No. 46243 *City of Lancaster* restarts the northbound 'Royal Scot' after pausing to take up the Beattock banker. A 10-mile ascent follows at

grades of mostly 1 in 75. The Caledonian main line then strides across the Central Lowlands to Stirling, Perth and Aberdeen, with junctions at Carstairs for Edinburgh and at Motherwell for Glasgow.

(Ronald Toop, August 1959)

Britain's last steam main line was Waterloo to Weymouth, ending in July 1967. It was the preserve of the Southern Pacifics of which 140 were built between 1941 and 1951, 30 as 'Merchant Navy' class and 110 as the lighter 'West Country/Battle of Britain' class. Originally with air-smoothed casings and chain-driven valve gear, 90 were rebuilt between 1957 and 1961 to improve reliability and maintenance. In a delightful cutting with spring flowers, rebuilt light Pacific No. 34090 *Sir Eustace Missenden, Southern Railway* heads a Down Bournemouth express on the approach to Shawford (north of Eastleigh).

(*Alan Postlethwaite, 20.5.61*)

The class A2 Pacifics was introduced by the LNER in 1943 and forty were built. Their design was developed in stages – first, rebuilds of 2–8–2 class P2, followed by a version with V2 boilers, a Thompson variation with an entirely new boiler, Peppercorn's design with a slightly shorter wheel-base and finally, a batch with double chimneys. No. 60537 *Bachelor's Button* is the penultimate version (postwar, single chimney), seen here departing Edinburgh through Princes Street Gardens with an Aberdeen train. *Bachelor's Button* (a common name for the buttercup) was a champion racehorse in the early twentieth century.

(Ronald Toop, August 1958)

Class A4 Pacific No. 60029 *Woodcock* makes a fine sight emerging from Stoke Tunnel with the Up 'Norseman' – the 12.10 Newcastle Tyne Commission Quay to King's Cross. There were thirty-five locomotives in this class, introduced by Sir Nigel Gresley in 1935. Changes from the A3 design included higher steam pressure, cylinder and piston valve improvements, plus streamlining. Inspired by the German fast diesel service between Berlin and Hamburg, the A4s headed the LNER's prestige 'Silver Jubilee' express service which enabled Newcastle businessmen to visit London for the day.

(Hugh Ballantyne, 19.8.61)

Climbing the upper Clyde Valley near Crawford on a lovely autumn afternoon, 'Princess Coronation' class Pacific No. 46251 *City of Nottingham* hauls a returning excursion from Glasgow Central to Nottingham. (This locomotive can also be seen at Swindon on p. 108.) There were thirty-eight engines in the class, introduced by Sir William Stanier in 1937 as a development of the 'Princess Royal'. Used principally on the West Coast main line, the streamlined version headed the 'Coronation Scot' service of pre-war days, inspiring that well-known piece of music by Vivian Ellis (1904–96). Can you hear the violins?

(Hugh Ballantyne, 5.10.63)

II

CROSS-COUNTRY AND SECONDARY SERVICES

The Midland & South Western Junction Railway provided access between the Midlands and Southampton independent of the Great Western. There were through coaches from the north and through freight to Southampton docks. In 1923, the Great Western absorbed the M&SWJR and services terminated latterly at Cheltenham St James. Arriving at Andoversford, Churchward Mogul No. 6387 lays a generous trail of smoke with the 2.00 p.m. Cheltenham to Southampton.

(Hugh Ballantyne, 7.9.55)

This chapter looks at a selection of cross-country trains, together with secondary (stopping) services on main lines plus some long-distance routes across remote areas of Scotland, Wales and Northern Ireland. Train lengths vary from three to ten coaches. There might be through coaches from the Metropolis, remnants of what started as an express service but downgraded with distance to secondary and even branch status (e.g. the 'Atlantic Coast Express'). It was so much more civilized, comfortable and satisfying to complete one's journey in the same coach than to change trains, particularly for those with families and luggage. It was also thrilling to be uncoupled and shunted en route, providing renewed interest on a long, tiring journey.

While cross-country passenger services were sometimes as lengthy as main line express services, they were generally slower, calling at more stations and with generous allowances for connections. Because of their dependence upon connections and having to find paths on different regional lines, they were also prone to unpunctuality. Their fascination derives from the unusual routes (sometimes single-track) and from the diversity of locomotives and carriages which could be found on particular trains.

The 'Withered Arm' of the LSWR (west of Exeter) had 'four fingers and a thumb' serving Ilfracombe, Torrington, Bude, Padstow and Plymouth. They were served by local trains and by sections of the 'Atlantic Coast Express' out of Waterloo. SR Bulleid coaches were commonplace, as were standard 2–6–4 tanks during the latter days of steam. On a very cold, raw morning at Okehampton, No. 80037 creates clouds of steam as it waits to restart a local train bound for either Plymouth or Padstow. Although steel-clad, Bulleid steam stock had a wooden body with a canvas roof.

(David Hucknall, 4.4.64)

Many such services were seasonal, serving great holiday resorts throughout the UK, e.g. Birmingham New Street to Clacton-on-Sea, and Newcastle Central to Blackpool. Other trains were 'specials', for football matches and national events. There were also cross-country freight trains, for both general goods and minerals for specific industries, e.g. iron ore transported from the East Midlands to South Wales.

Some secondary services were over the 'main lines' of relatively small pre-Group companies like the North Staffordshire, the Furness, the Cambrian, the Cheshire Lines Committee and the Great North of Scotland Railway – fine companies but serving limited geographic areas (except for through services). Some small railways were jointly owned, including the M&GN (Midland and Great Northern), the M&SWJ (Midland and South Western Junction), the Somerset & Dorset (joint Midland/LSWR) and Shrewsbury to South Wales (joint GWR/LNWR). More usually, however, cross-country services made straight connections between companies; for Brighton and the Kent Coast, for example, inter-company connections were made at Salisbury, Reading or Kensington Olympia, sometimes with engine changes but often running through with a 'foreigner', adding further interest for the enthusiast.

So many cross-country lines and services are now extinct, following a decline which was begun by the Big Four. The decline was arrested during the Second World War but was pursued with renewed vigour by Dr Beeching and his successors. As services were wound down to the point of extinction, there were many cries of 'foul' from enthusiasts and users. BR was accused of making cross-country lines uneconomic by withdrawing or diverting key services and connections, so that what service remained was not worth using. The M&SWJR, for example, finished with just one daily through passenger train from Cheltenham Spa to Southampton, with no connection from the Midlands and with no through service in the reverse direction. What the railway management was actually doing was accelerating what was seen as the inevitable – complete withdrawals and closures in the face of the growing use of cars and lorries, especially on the new motorways. The competition was viewed as inexorable and overwhelming.

Whereas many of the 'express' classes of locomotives in the first chapter were Pacifics (4–6–2 wheel arrangement), the classes in this chapter are predominantly 4–6–0, an arrangement originally developed for express passenger duty but here applied to secondary work. Apart from 'ten-wheeler' in the US, it is strange that no common name has been given to the 4–6–0 wheel arrangement. Terms like 'Atlantic' and 'Pacific', which came from the US railroads that first adopted them, became common in the UK. A suitable 4–6–0 name would have been the 'Churchward' or the 'Western', in recognition of the Great Western's Locomotive Superintendent who developed the 4–6–0 as a UK standard. This was achieved during the early 1900s as part of extensive investigations and trials, not only into wheel arrangements but into cylinder arrangements (simple versus compound expansion, 2 versus 4 cylinders), cylinder design (long-stroke), valve gear design (long-travel, long-lap) and high boiler pressure (225 p.s.i.). The trials were conducted against a batch of de Glehn compound Atlantics imported from France, then the epitome of express passenger design. As a result, George Churchward developed a series of simple 'standard' designs which matched the efficiency of the de Glehn Atlantics while avoiding their complexity of compounding. The principles thus established endured for the remaining life of the Great Western and spread to other major railways, especially to the LMS under Stanier (an ex-GWR man) and to BR under Riddles (ex-GWR and LMS). This chapter includes 4–6–0 examples from each of the Big Four and from BR.

Railway photographs in the snow are rare, not least because the extremities of the photographer tend to get frozen! Towards the end of the 'Great Freeze' of 1962, a train to Wolverhampton and beyond is headed by an unidentified 4–6–0, a mile or so south of Stafford. It could be a cross-country service to Bristol or a semi-fast to Birmingham. Quite remarkable is the cleanliness of the LMS coaches, nicely reflecting the snow from both windows and bodywork. After walking on to Penkridge, the frozen photographer sought refuge in the relative warmth of a Midland Red bus.

(Alan Postlethwaite, 3.3.62)

The Midland & Great Northern Joint Railway provided the only serious challenge to the Great Eastern's monopoly of East Anglia. There were services to Norwich, Great Yarmouth and Cromer from London and the Midlands, and important holiday traffic was developed between the Midlands and the coast. Here, at Sutton Bridge, the 11.10 a.m. Yarmouth Beach to Leicester is double-headed by Fowler 0–6–0 class 4F Nos 43954 and 44231. This class was introduced by the Midland Railway in 1911 for freight, and construction was perpetuated by the LMS until 1940.

(Hugh Ballantyne, 30.8.58)

Although designated 'main line' by the Cambrian Railways Company, the 95-mile line from Whitchurch to Aberystwyth was 'secondary' by national standards. Just south of Llanymynech, GWR Mogul No. 7313 has entered a single-track section with a Down 3-coacher and is about to cross the River Vyrnwy into Wales. Just behind the train, the Llanfyllin branch goes off to the left on what was originally part of the Potteries, Shrewsbury & North Wales Railway, later becoming the Shropshire & Montgomeryshire Railway under Colonel Stephens. All lines from Llanymynech are now closed.

(Alan Postlethwaite, 9.6.62)

The familiar outline of Edinburgh Waverley is the setting for a pair of lovely LNER engines. Thompson 4–6–0 class B1 No. 61197 is ready to depart with the 10.40 a.m. to Dundee while Gresley 2–6–2 tank class V1 No. 67620 is on shunting duties with LNER East Coast stock (in crimson and cream). Both locomotives are remarkably clean, a credit to their respective sheds – Eastfield

(Glasgow) and Haymarket (Edinburgh). Class V1 was introduced in 1930 for suburban passenger duty, followed in 1939 by the V3 (slightly higher boiler pressure); a combined total of ninety-two were built.

(Hugh Ballantyne, 6.5.57)

The Somerset & Dorset line was at its most scenic over the Mendip Hills. Here in the north Somerset countryside at Midford, S&DJR 2–8–0 No. 53808 pilots BR 4–6–0 No. 73051 onto a double-track section with the 10.28 a.m. Manchester London Road to Bournemouth West, a relief train to the 'Pines Express'. Midford signal-box can be seen beyond the 170-yard long viaduct. This class was introduced in 1914 to the design of Sir Henry Fowler (Midland Railway). No. 53808 is preserved on the West Somerset Railway while No. 53809 is at the Midland Railway Centre near Ripley.

(Hugh Ballantyne, 15.8.59)

An evocative sight of a 'Manor' gleaming in the early spring sunlight in the fine setting of a small-town station on the Welsh borders. GWR 4–6–0 No. 7823 *Hook Norton Manor* takes water at Welshpool, working the Down 'Cambrian Coast Express', the 11.10 a.m. Paddington to Aberystwyth. This 'overview' of a clean engine brings out some distinctive features of the GWR family: twin whistles on the Belpaire firebox, brass cover for the safety valve and top feed, lack of dome on the taper boiler, and copper-topped chimney.

(Hugh Ballantyne, 31.3.62)

The railway promoted Oban as a fishing port, resort and gateway to the Isles. It was served by the Caledonian's long line across the southern Highlands from Stirling in the east. At Crianlarich, it junctioned with the West Highland line of the North British Railway (to Mallaig). After 1965, all Oban services ran via the NBR into Glasgow. Both lines had severe grades and some spectacular scenery. Here, in rugged moorland, LMS 4–6–0 class 5 No. 44921 brings a five-coach train down the final 1 in 50 bank towards Oban.

(Ronald Toop, August 1958)

Caledonian 0–6–0 tank class '782' No. 56291 pilots a long train of empty stock at Inverness. This was the hub of the Highland Railway system, with lines radiating to Keith, Perth, Kyle of Lochalsh and Wick/Thurso. The great signal gantry guards the eastern approach to the Inverness triangle, with the station round to the left from Welsh's Bridge signal-box. This class of engine was introduced by J.F. McIntosh in 1895 for freight and shunting and a total of 357 were built; it has design similarities to the 'Caley' 0–4–4 tank (pp. 48, 90).

(Ronald Toop, August 1958)

The Highland Railway meanders north from Inverness for some 150 miles to Wick, with a branch to Britain's most northerly station at Thurso (for Orkney). To alight there is like arriving in Scandinavia. The termini at Wick and Thurso are similar, having a wooden overall roof just long enough to cover the engine and first coach. Here at Thurso, Stanier 2–6–2 tank class 3MT No. 40150 stands ready to depart with the 3.40 p.m. to Inverness, but the locomotive will work only as far as Georgmas Junction where the coaches will attach to the portion from Wick.

(Hugh Ballantyne, 2.5.57)

Stanier class 5MT was introduced by the LMS in 1934 and 842 were built. They were derived from the earlier 'Jubilee' class but with smaller driving wheels and only two cylinders. Commonly known as 'Black Fives', they could be found throughout the LMS system and despite their huge population, sturdy good looks made them a favourite with enthusiasts. Here at Aberdeen station, No. 44998 sits at the head of empty stock in ex-works condition, spending a few days 'running in' after overhaul at Inverurie works. Its home depot was Perth (63A).

(Brian J. Dickson, 26.4.65)

Buttington was the junction of Cambrian 'main line' with the important GWR/LMS (joint) connecting line from Shrewsbury (coming in here from the right). Issuing much steam from the exhaust, safety valve and around the cylinder, standard 4–6–0 class 4 No. 75005 comes through non-stop with the 9.45 Whitchurch to Aberystwyth, passing GWR 0–6–0 No. 3207 waiting by the

signal-box with a Permanent Way train. The latter class comprised 120 engines and was introduced by C.B. Collett in 1930 for light freight and passenger duties. Its taper boiler is dwarfed by that of the larger, higher-set class 4.

(Hugh Ballantyne, 5.3.56)

One of the most attractive lineside points for photography must be this approach to Bradford-on-Avon. Coming down the avenue is GWR 4–6–0 No. 5937 *Stanford Hall* with the 12.26 to Portsmouth. The lower quadrant signal is set for the 12.30 from Bradford-on-Avon to Cardiff, a service handled almost exclusively by 'Halls' but soon to be monopolized by 'Hymek' diesel-hydraulics. This line handled all the Bristol to Weymouth traffic and was a relief route for Bath to Chippenham. There was also much coal traffic until the demise of the South Wales and Somerset coalfields.

(Revd Alan Newman, 28.3.63)

The LSWR introduced 4–6–0 class N15 in 1918 to the design of Robert Urie. Its design was subsequently improved to become the Southern's well-loved 'King Arthur' class. No. 30769 *Sir Balan* is seen here approaching Canterbury East with an Up semi-fast from Dover. The scene is enhanced by the lone photographer in the goods yard and by the magnificent stilted LCDR signal-box.

(Alan Postlethwaite, 29.3.59)

Class S 4–4–0 No. 170, formerly *Errigal*, stands in Strabane station with the fireman watching for the 'right away'. It is working the 10.15 from Londonderry (Foyle Road) to Belfast (Great Victoria Street) on the GNR(I) route via Omagh. Just five of this class were built by Beyer Peacock in 1913 and renewed in Dundalk in 1939. On the breakup of the GNR in 1958, this locomotive went south to the CIE but returned north after CIE dieselization in 1963. Sister engine No. 171 is preserved.

(Hugh Ballantyne, 2.9.64)

Level crossings are commonplace on the flat lands of the east of England. This one is for farm traffic at the east end of Luffington station on the Midland line from Peterborough to Stamford. The approaching train is headed by standard class 5 No. 75060 – crisp, clean and gleaming in the winter sunshine.

(Alan Postlethwaite, 20.3.63)

Barnwell station stands on the LNWR line from Northampton to Peterborough. Arriving with a west-bound train is LNER 4–6–0 class B1 No. 61059. Also known as 'Antelopes', this mixed traffic class was introduced by Edward Thompson in 1942 to replace some twenty-one older classes of 4–6–0. Because of wartime restrictions on tooling and machining, it was designed to incorporate standard parts of other classes including the 'Sandringham' boiler, K2 cylinders and V2 wheels. Unlike the original Frankenstein, the B1 was an instant and enduring success.

(Alan Postlethwaite, 22.3.63)

III

BRANCH LINES AND NARROW GAUGE

Plenty of activity at Launceston follows the arrival of the 10.40 a.m. from Plymouth North Road. GWR Prairie tank No. 5567 takes water as another locomotive attaches to the rear. On platform 2, a stack of mail bags and a gaggle of passengers await the arrival of a train to Exeter. This LSWR through station also became the terminal for Plymouth trains following the closure in 1952 of Tavistock's GWR branch terminus.

(Hugh Ballantyne, 20.12.55)

To complete our initial journey, we must change onto a branch line. Typically, this might be served by a couple of coaches plus tank-engine, perhaps fitted for push–pull operation, running over some 5 miles of lightly-laid track, often with relatively severe grades and curves, to a modest terminus of one platform, a bay and a small goods yard. In reality, there were many variations on this model, including double-ended branches (no terminus), double-track branches (often to towns which had originally rejected railways), goods-only lines (to serve specific industries), tender engines and some very long branches which were isolated by geography (mountains, sea inlets etc.).

The main points of interest on branches were the junction and the terminus. This was where the action was – watering, coaling, running round, picking up vans and coaches, passenger movements, meetings and greetings, busy railwaymen and connections with main line trains, local buses and taxis. By comparison, intermediate stations on branches could be sleepy but picturesque. Intermediate scenery could be beautiful, sometimes spectacular, as the branch curved and climbed steeply through terrain that no heavy train could hope to conquer.

Our pictures are dominated by the Great Western, regarded by many as having the most picturesque of

The simple but attractive GWR branch terminus at Ashburton has inspired many modellers, including the Revd Peter Denny with his renowned 'Buckingham Great Central' of 1950s vintage. Brunel's overall roof covers the platforms for passengers (left) and parcels (right). There were also sidings serving the goods shed, a malt house and the locomotive shed. Collett 0–4–2 tank No. 1470 stands ready to depart with the 3.35 p.m. to Totnes. Two of this class (Nos 1420 and 1450) are preserved on a 7-mile section of this branch, based at Buckfastleigh and known today as the South Devon Railway.

(Hugh Ballantyne, 14.8.56)

the branch lines. They were popular too with modellers and, during the 1960s, journals like the *Railway Modeller* were sometimes upbraided for giving undue coverage to GWR branches. One can only use what is offered, however, and the GW branch remains the most popular, as reflected in this chapter.

Another feature of the pictures is that all the locomotive designs originated in the pre-nationalization era. Branch lines were the last hunting grounds of so many classes of small engine which had previously experienced more intense activity on suburban or mixed traffic duties. There were exceptions to this pattern, including the 2–4–0 and 0–4–2 tanks which were designed specifically for light branch service. Some branches were privileged with new BR tanks, but the older engines always seemed more at home on branch lines.

Several of the trains pictured here were fitted for push–pull operation (also known as 'auto-trains'). This practice evolved from the 'rail-motor', a small tank engine integral with a coach, in the early twentieth century, as a means of reducing operating costs on branch services. The rail-motor, however, was difficult for maintenance and availability and all were subsequently converted to auto-trains. The Big Four all used auto-trains to a greater or lesser extent, and BR continued to build them, usually as conversions from old main line stock.

Another economy measure was to build branch lines as 'light railways'. Although this limited the axle weight and speed of trains, it was an effective means of reducing both capital and running costs. Mixed passenger/freight trains were a particular feature of such lines. Colonel Holman H. Stephens was a great advocate of the light railway, and from 1892 until his death in 1931 he built, operated and

owned a small empire of little lines nationwide. Thereafter, they gradually declined and closed but some are preserved, including the delightful Kent & East Sussex Railway based at Tenterden.

Another form of low-cost light railway was the narrow gauge line. This was particularly suited to serve quarries in mountainous terrain or to serve communities in isolated areas. As they generally ran through beautiful scenery, many have survived as tourist railways and are represented in this chapter by the the Isle of Man Railway. Of all the branches and light railways built, the narrow gauge achieved that intriguing sense of running along grassy paths through people's back gardens. With the locomotive making steam, they could be very picturesque!

Most branches were instigated and financed by local business interests and were built independently before being absorbed by an established railway company just before or within a few years of opening. Many were never economic but were nevertheless taken over, simply to keep a rival company at bay. Some branches remained independent until the Grouping of 1923 or nationalization in 1948. Even then, hundreds of short industrial branches remained independent of BR.

One of the dilemmas of the branch line builders was to what extent they should allow for future traffic growth. There are examples of provision for doubling the track, for expansion of terminal facilities and for extension to the 'far and beyond'. Some local companies were bold enough to build double-track from the outset, often leading to a grand terminus. We remain indebted to all the Victorian branch line builders who speculated their wealth in order to open up some of the UK's most beautiful countryside to railway traffic.

In the southern foothills of the Peak District, Norbury station nestles in the lower Dove Valley. This was part of the North Staffordshire Railway's branch to Ashbourne where it made an end-on junction with the LNWR branch from Buxton. There were once through services between Buxton and Uttoxeter. The shortest goods train of the week comprised a single coal truck plus brake van, headed by LMS 2–6–4 tank No. 42609. On the return journey, the train length increased to four vans and a five-plank truck.

(Alan Postlethwaite, 5.5.62)

The Manx Northern Railway was opened in 1879, remaining independent for a quarter of a century until taken over by the Isle of Man Railway in 1904. It provided a roundabout route from Douglas to Ramsey. North of St John's and climbing onto the boggy moors of the west coast, a mixed train to Ramsey is headed by 2–4–0 tank No. 8 *Fenella*. Gravity shunting was practised to dispose of the odd truck en route. *Fenella* entered service in 1894 during the most prosperous era of Man's railways.

(Alan Postlethwaite, 1.9.60)

On a North British branch line through Roxboroughshire, LNER 0–6–0 class J39 No. 64917 trundles through Maxton station with the daily local goods train of bottom hopper and open mineral wagons. This was a cross-border service from Tweedsmouth to St Boswells where it joined the 'Waverley' route to Edinburgh. The line started as North Eastern Railway, becoming North British at an end-on junction 1¼ miles east of Kelso. This class of 289 locomotives was introduced by Sir Nigel Gresley in 1926; although intended for freight, appearances on passenger trains became increasingly common during the 1930s.

(Hugh Ballantyne, 26.8.60)

A morning departure at Llanfyllin in the heart of Montgomeryshire, as LMS Mogul No. 46509 heads a passenger service to the junction at Llanymynech. The train is nicely framed by the tubular GWR signal gantry, plus the hut, water tower and telegraph pole – the sort of idyllic setting that modellers strive to achieve. The unused land on the left suggests provision for future growth of

services and facilities. The branch was opened in 1863 by the Cambrian Railways and endured without significant change for just over a century.

(Alan Postlethwaite, 9.6.62)

The 10-mile, double-track Windermere branch left the Lancaster & Carlisle main line (LNWR) at Oxenholme. It was an early branch, opening in 1846–7 after opposition led by William Wordsworth. Having the unashamed purpose of promoting tourism, the modern town of Windermere grew from this splendid terminus which once stood isolated by the lakeside. Aspirations to extend the line to Keswick were never realized. LMS 2–6–4 tank class 4MT No. 42299 stands at Windermere with a long local train for Kendal and Oxenholme. Note the end-windows at the guard's end of the LMS coaches.

(Ronald Toop, August 1963)

The Great Western line through Stroud had a triple personality with fast trains from Paddington, stopping trains from Swindon and auto-trains from Gloucester serving the 'Golden Valley'. Collett 0–4–2 tank No. 1458 restarts a 'branch' service from Brimscombe towards Chalford. The engine shed alongside was of curious design, having an integral water tower. It was the home of the 'Brimscombe banker', in this case GWR 4–6–0 No. 7815 *Fritwell Manor*, ready for its next turn up the Sapperton bank.

(Revd Alan Newman, 25.8.64)

A Cambrian Railways branch. The railway blends beautifully with the pastures, farmhouse and gentle hills of the Cambrian countryside near Bryngwyn on the Llanfyllin branch. This east-bound train is headed by Ivatt class 2MT Mogul No. 46509, a class of 128 introduced by the LMS in 1946 and perpetuated virtually unchanged as a BR standard design. Few CR engines had survived up to nationalization and it is a little sad that the branch did not see out its days with GWR engines.

(Alan Postlethwaite, 9.6.62)

The Taff Vale Railway is best known for suing its employees' trades union for strike damages, a consequence of which was the birth of the Labour Party. An early railway, opening in 1840–1, it was grouped with the GWR in 1923. Its hub was Pontypridd, at the confluence of the Taff and Rhonda valleys. GWR Pannier tank No. 6417, recently transferred from Laira to Aberdare shed, waits at Pontypridd with a Sunday afternoon auto-train, ready for a trip up the TVR branch to Aberdare Low Level. Colliers no doubt inhabit the terraced cottages on the hillside.

(Maurice Dart, 9.6.57)

St John's was once the seat of the Tynwald, the Isle of Man's parliament. It also boasted the island's only junction station. Locomotive No. 5 *Mona* has just arrived with a pair of banana-shaped coaches from Ramsey, while No. 8 *Fenella* has uncoupled from its single coach from Peel. The train on the left has meanwhile arrived from Douglas. The right-hand line once continued

southwards to the lead-mining community of Foxdale, rising mostly at 1 in 49 and crossing the Douglas line by a bridge just east of here. The Foxdale branch closed in about 1940 and St John's closed in 1965.

(Alan Postlethwaite, 2.9.60)

The Teign Valley line opened from Heathfield to Ashton in 1882 and through to Exeter in 1903. It junctioned with the Moretenhampstead branch at Heathfield, thereby creating (theoretically) a relief route for services between Exeter and Newton Abbot. It was an archetypal GWR country branch, albeit double-ended. Arriving at Christow with the 12.49 from Heathfield to Exeter is a smart train headed by 0–4–2 tank No. 1451 in lined green. Introduced by C.B. Collett in 1932, there were seventy-five locomotives in the class.

(Hugh Ballantyne, 15.2.58)

Churchward's preference for the Belpaire firebox (squarish) led to the development of the Pannier in preference to the Saddle tank. Between 1903 and 1949, well over a thousand GWR Panniers were built for shunting and light freight. Also used on branches, No. 6400 is standing with auto-trailer W230W at Tavistock, ready to depart with the 12.35 to Plymouth North Road (via Yelverton). Tavistock was nearly halfway up the Great Western's Launceston branch, completed in 1865.

(Hugh Ballantyne, 8.8.61)

I V

FOCUS ON FREIGHT, PARCELS AND INDUSTRY

Ivatt Mogul class 2MT No. 46401 approaches the 10 m.p.h. speed restriction on the 'Midland platform' at Huntingdon East, heading a fruit train for the northern markets. Owing to line weight restrictions, double-heading was not allowed between Huntingdon East and St Ives. A Midland 0–6–0 class 2F would shortly be attached, however, to pilot the train over the steeply graded continuation to Kettering. The 'Midland platform' closed in 1957.

(Eric Sawford, 9.7.53)

Mineral traffic has always been a mainstay of railway revenues. The very first railways were built for mining and quarrying, originally horse-drawn but converting to steam, mostly as short connections to the established waterways. As railways expanded to serve towns and cities, so railway traffic expanded to include passengers, parcels, agricultural products and general goods. All types of rail traffic grew, creating conflicting demands on main lines between fast passenger services on the one hand and comparatively slow freight on the other. New goods loops were added, some lines were quadrupled and central marshalling yards were built. New industries sprang up alongside the railway lines, sometimes with great networks of private sidings. Many railways moved their 'works' from restricted city sites to more spacious 'country' junctions, thereby transforming small villages into new industrial towns. Major ports were developed from small harbours to take advantage of the railway connection, cutting overall journey times and costs, and creating new international trade links.

During the reign of steam, freight accounted for some two-thirds of railway revenues and for most of the profits. This was because industries tended to operate throughout the year with fairly steady and predictable flows of raw materials and products. Principal freight trains therefore ran full or nearly so, and could be scheduled to avoid the peak flows of passenger traffic. Freight was a high volume, steady and profitable business. Passenger traffic, on the other hand, was 'unstorable', less predictable and more 'peaky', both diurnally and seasonally. A large reserve of coaches was required to cater for the peaks of daily rush hours and annual holidays, but the annual 'load factor' of passenger traffic was inherently poor, with many trains running half-empty or less. What is more, the travelling public demanded fast, regular, punctual, clean and 'friendly' services. Managing a passenger service was like riding a tiger – a balance of nerve, skill and an element of good fortune.

R.J. Essery *et al* (*British Goods Wagons from 1887 to Present*, David & Charles, 1970) quotes company sources for a breakdown of the British wagon fleet at the time of nationalization. Out of nearly 1¼ million vehicles, mineral wagons accounted for 56 per cent, followed by open goods (26 per cent), covered goods (12 per cent) and others (6 per cent). These totals include nearly half a million former private-owner wagons which were taken over by the Big Four in 1939; many had been colliery owned, adding much colour and interest to local coal yards (both real and in model form). Most pre-nationalization wagons were 'unfitted' wooden 4-wheelers to a wheel base of 10 or 12 ft, with capacities in the range 8–20 tons. Under BR, steel replaced wooden construction, capacities were increased and more vehicles were 'pipe-fitted' for continuous braking (to achieve higher speeds). The BR 16-ton steel mineral wagon became commonplace, followed by the 25-ton bottom-hopper wagon used on 'merry-go-round' trains.

During the last years of steam, freight still dominated. *Modern Railways* (March 1963) quotes BR traffic receipts for 1962 as follows: passengers (35 per cent), coal and coke (23 per cent), other minerals (8 per cent), goods (21 per cent) and parcels by passenger train (13 per cent). At this time, the nation was dependent upon coal for over 90 per cent of its energy needs, with uses ranging from power stations, gas works, iron and steel production, domestic hearths to the railways themselves. Some lines saw an endless succession of heavy coal trains, like a pipeline but with flexibility of sources and destinations. Such traffic has continued, together with the bulk carrying of limestone, iron ore, china clay, compacted refuse, nuclear flasks, automotive products, petro-chemicals and cement. General goods, on the other hand, have declined to long-distance container traffic, and most of the great marshalling yards are now redundant.

Our pictures show a representative selection of different types of freight train – fast long-distance 'perishables', loose-coupled local pick-ups, minerals and coal, open goods, mixed goods, covered goods, (early) containers, and parcels, both bogie and

4-wheel. Locomotive types range between the 0–6–0, 2–6–0, 4–6–0 and 2–10–0, depending upon the train weight. Nearly all the moving trains are creating impressive displays of smoke and steam, indicative of the hard work being undertaken.

Mention is needed of the traditional organization and infrastructure needed to handle freight. A goods agent would manage a depot and keep abreast of local business activities and market opportunities. His chief clerk would supervise all paperwork and canvassing activities, as well as managing the cartage department, a fleet of lorries. Also under the agent, his inspector would supervise the railway staff of foremen, shunters, checkers, loaders, porters, number takers and labellers, etc. Consignments of goods started with local carting – it was a door-to-door service. Loading was done at the local goods yard with sidings, sheds, docks, end-loading ramp, cranes, etc., depending on local needs. The pick-up goods train would deposit wagons at the nearest junction station or specialist yard for marshalling into longer trains to distant destinations. Central freight depots in cities could be huge, with Goliath travelling cranes and covered accommodation for wagons, platforms and lorries, plus an army of railwaymen to handle a continuous stream of comings and goings. Goods were loaded, unloaded, transhipped and stored at the major depots. Covered wagons would be sealed and trains would then be marshalled for departure at scheduled times.

Started by the Big Four and continued by BR, freight modernization included mechanization of goods depots, the upgrading of 'hump' yards with automatically controlled wagon retarders, and the replacement of the old small-capacity wagons with larger modern wagons. Despite these noble efforts, or perhaps because of them where industries were coerced into modernization, rail freight traffic declined as general goods defected to new roads, motorways and the juggernaut. The last days of steam therefore witness some of the last days of local general freight. The small yard and the loose-coupled pick-up goods train have gone forever.

The daily goods arrives at the mid-Wales branch terminus of Llanfyllin and will now exchange a wagon or two before returning to the Cambrian 'main line' at Llanymynech. Unashamedly functional, the large water tank, modest bunker, dome of the scoop fountain (for water troughs) and water filler show clearly on the tender of LMS class 2F Mogul No. 46519. The multi-level tender, together with the small diameter boiler and large cab, give this class a 'Continental' appearance.

(Alan Postlethwaite, 9.6.62)

The Cambridge to March 'loop line' via St Ives opened in 1848 and was used latterly by many freight trains to avoid Ely. An 0–6–0 class J17 No. 65554 heads for its home depot at March, seen here passing St Ives with a mixed goods train. Introduced in 1901 to the design of J. Holden, a total of ninety were built for freight. A characteristic was the low-pitch boiler which made the cab seem exceptionally large.

(Eric Sawford, 23.5.53)

Near Wedgwood Halt, LMS 'Crab' No. 42887 runs tender first in winter sunshine up the Trent Valley line with a long train of empty coal wagons. This class 6P/5F Mogul was designed by George Hughes (ex-Lancashire & Yorkshire Railway) under the direction of Sir Henry Fowler. A total of 245 were built between 1926 and 1932 and could be found throughout the LMS system. Their appearance was unique with such huge cylinders (21 in in diameter) and a bi-level running plate.

(Alan Postlethwaite, 17.3.62)

A lively goods train threads its way between fields in the lower reaches of Dove Dale on the Uttoxeter to Leek line of the former North Staffordshire Railway, near the junction for the Ashbourne branch. Headed by Fairburn class 4MT 2–6–4 tank No. 42663, the train includes a wooden truck, a small steel hopper and an assortment of vans. The framework of leafless branches brings a sense of chill to this spring scene, relieved only by the exhaust steam and the level-crossing.

(Alan Postlethwaite, 14.4.62)

The signalman's car is a sign of the times at Charwelton on the Great Central line in Northamptonshire where the goods yard is in the process of demolition. This station is typical of the last main line to London (opened in 1899), comprising an island platform below a road bridge, with provision for quadrupling that never happened. Bringing life to the scene is standard 2–10–0 class 9F

No. 92013 with a Down freight, mostly coal. Freight provided most of the workings hereabouts at this time, including iron ore from Charwelton quarries.

(Revd Alan Newman, 7.10.64)

Bass 0–4–0 saddle tank No. 7 shunting at Shobnall Wharf sidings, Burton-on-Trent. It was built in 1875 by Thornewill & Wareham (works No. 400) as a well tank, but was later rebuilt by Hunslet Engine Co. Several thousand saddle tanks were employed at various periods throughout British industry in collieries, power stations, docks and the steel industry. Bass alone had fourteen from the above-named maker.

(Maurice Dart, 16.9.58)

As a PR exercise during the late 1950s, a selection of tank engines were repainted and designated as 'station pilots' at certain principal locations. This is class J72 0–6–0 tank No. 68736 at York, resplendent in North Eastern Railway livery and sporting the NER crest on its tanks. It belongs to the original batch of eighty-five shunting engines introduced by Wilson Worsdell in 1898. (A second batch of twenty-eight to the same design was built by BR in 1950–1.) Note the distinctive design of the SR utility van on the left; they wandered all over Britain.

(Maurice Dart, 13.8.60)

Opposite: Worsdell 0–6–0 class J27 No. 65815 blasts its way out of New Bridge Street Goods Yard (Newcastle) with a hopper train, climbing towards Jesmond and Gosforth South junction. This North Blyth-based engine was built for the NER in 1908 by the North British Locomotive Co. Renowned for 'robust and unflagging hard work on local mineral traffic' (*Locomotives of the LNER Pt. 5*, RCTS, 1984), all 115 of the class entered BR service, but only 36 remained by June 1966. The goods depot opened in the early 1900s, suffered considerable air-raid damage in 1941 and closed in 1967.

(David Hucknall, November 1965)

Stafford was a major centre for both passenger traffic and freight. The latter is emphasized here in the reception sidings and marshalling yard (left), local goods depot, sidings and No. 2 signal-box (right) and the quadruple main line (centre) guarded by a fine pair of LNWR wooden gantries. 'Black Five' No. 45441 heads a train of container wagons out of Stafford station and is signalled to proceed on the Up fast line towards Rugby. The end is nigh for these grand old signals, for their diminutive replacement colour-lights can be seen in the foreground.

(Alan Postlethwaite, 8.4.62)

The locomotive fleet of the NCC was dramatically improved in 1933 when class W Moguls were introduced. No. 91 *The Bush* is shunting at Strabane during the course of working a Londonderry to Portadown goods. This mixed traffic class was based on the Fowler LMS 2–6–4 tank but with slightly larger (6 ft diameter) wheels. The first four came assembled from Derby but the remaining eleven were constructed at York Road Works, Belfast. The original straight-sided Fowler tenders were replaced with larger Stanier tenders, seen here. Note the tablet apparatus attached to the cab.

(Hugh Ballantyne, 4.9.64)

At Portadown, 0–6–0 class UG No. 48 acts as station pilot on a train of 4-wheel wooden vans, while a DMU on the left works the Belfast to Newry service. There were ten engines in class UG, with five built in Dundalk in 1937 and five by Beyer Peacock in 1947. This engine was originally No. 146 of the GNR(I) but became No. 48 as one of five absorbed into the UTA system in 1948. Although designed for goods, their short wheel base and 15½-ton axle weight gave them complete system availability for general purposes.

(Hugh Ballantyne, 3.9.64)

Gresley's 0–6–0 class J38 was introduced by the LNER in 1926 for freight duty and thirty-five were built. Here in the sidings at East Leith is No. 65912, allocated to St Margaret's shed. The 'New Leith Line' was built by the Caledonian Railway in the 1880s to exploit the opening of Edinburgh Dock. A cold spell has left the grass and van roofs thickly coated with frost. Goods traffic was still sufficient to justify a daily visit from a shunting engine, handling such diverse products as Crawford's biscuits and liquid ammonia from SAI Ltd.

(David Hucknall, 19.1.65)

The bunker of this Caledonian 0–4–4 tank looks massive. The class was introduced by J.F. MacIntosh in 1895 for suburban passenger duties, but became a mainstay for branch duties. Many were latterly fitted with stovepipe chimneys (see p. 90) but not No. 55260, seen here at Beattock with a brake van in the platform formerly used by trains for the Moffat branch. Production was continued (with variations) from 1915 under W. Pickersgill and a total of 146 were built.

(Ronald Toop, August 1958)

Just north of Stratford, nestling in the marshes of the Lea Valley, lies the mechanized marshalling yard of Temple Mills. The actuator of a retarder can been seen in the foreground, one of eight feeding a fan of forty-seven sorting sidings for wagons which have been propelled over the hump by a diesel. Passing in the Down direction with a wonderful collection of loaded coal wagons is a Great Eastern 0–6–0 class J17 whose number looks like 65528. A crewman is visible through the side-window.

(Alan Postlethwaite, 1.11.58)

The LNWR had two important routes from Crewe/Chester to South Wales – either via the Shrewsbury & Hereford line (joint GWR/LNWR) or from a junction on the latter at Craven Arms across Radnor and Brecknock to Carmarthen and Swansea (mostly LNWR). A long fitted freight of assorted vans is bound for South Wales, photographed at Dorrington, two stations south of Shrewsbury, headed by GWR 4–6–0 No. 6928 *Underley Hall*.

(Alan Postlethwaite, 19.6.62)

Near Coventry on the main line to Birmingham, LMS class 5MT No. 45276 heads a short parcels train on a murky winter's morning. The scene is brought to life by the fine semaphore signals, so tall and vivid on their gantry that the train is dwarfed almost to insignificance. The sense of height is echoed by the line of telegraph poles on the right and by the leafless trees beyond. The signals guard the junction for the line to Nuneaton which branches to the left of this picture.

(Alan Postlethwaite, 18.2.62)

By 1964, most of the passenger services on the West Coast main line were diesel-hauled, but a large fleet of LMS class 5MT and 8F steam engines were still very much in evidence on goods trains, albeit usually in a grimy condition. On a typically dull and overcast summer's day on the Cumberland Fells, a dirty 4–6–0 class 5 No. 45096 hauls a Down fitted freight past Shap Wells, banked by class 4 Tebay 2–6–4 tank No. 42110. This is three-quarters of the way up the 4-mile, 1 in 75 slog of Shap bank.

(Hugh Ballantyne, 29.8.64)

The West Coast main line in winter, with LMS class 5MT No. 45374 making a fine plume of steam at the head of a long freight train near Standon Bridge, north Staffordshire, on the Down fast line between Norton Bridge and Crewe. The discarded sleepers are evidence of recent work to install flat-bottom track, although not long-welded. Only the right-hand track is still bullhead. Work is also in progress for resignalling with colour-lights, a prelude to electrification.

(Hugh Ballantyne, 18.2.61)

V

ON SHED AND IN YARDS – THE STEAM LOCOMOTIVE

St Margaret's, Edinburgh, was a shed of great character, hemmed in at the eastern end of Waverley station. Its large steam stud had declined by the time of this picture. On a drizzly day, LNER engines (left to right) are A4 Pacific No. 60006 *Sir Ralph Wedgwood*, 2–6–2 class V2 No. 60813 with its odd modified chimney, and A3 Pacific No. 60100 *Spearmint*. A Clayton type 1 diesel lurks on the left.

(David Hucknall, April 1965)

The engine shed was where steam locomotives were kept, staffed, allocated to service, cleaned, turned, topped up with oil, grease, sand, coal and water, lit, heated, de-ashed, de-scaled, checked, logged, maintained and stored securely overnight, sometimes protected from the weather. In short, it was their operational base. In BR days, sheds were more correctly called Motive Power Depots or MPDs. They were located strategically to serve major termini, junctions and branch lines and to provide back-up engines in the event of failures in service. During the final decade of steam, there were over 400 MPDs in the UK, ranging from main sheds with a hundred or more allocations, to sub-sheds capable of holding a handful of engines or just one. The larger MPDs carried craftsmen and machine tools for routine repairs and maintenance, but major overhauls and rebuilds would be carried out at a central 'works'.

To the railway enthusiast, the engine shed was Mecca, a grimy Aladdin's cave where a fascinating assortment of locomotives lay hidden in the dim inner depths – locomotives of all shapes, sizes and ages, some obsolete, cold and rarely used, others warm and singing, awaited their next turn of duty. To visit a shed was like being offered the Crown Jewels, not knowing which to handle first. For some reason, engines collected together acquire 'added value', a phenomenon which can still be experienced to some extent in the National Railway Museum and in the sheds and sidings of the many preserved railways. In BR sheds, however, one was witnessing history as it happened, for one knew that within weeks, months or a few years, most of these lovely monsters would be scrapped. We were witnessing the approaching end of a dynasty, like the capping of the very last pyramid in Egypt, and this sense of history was always strongest in engine sheds.

Most sheds were haunted by the ghosts of railwaymen long past – drivers, firemen, cleaners, fitters, foremen, managers and engineer-designers. (There were also women there during the war years.) They are best sensed in quiet corners while standing unseen and unheard next to some massive driving wheels and cylinders or in a maintenance pit, perhaps. They were people who gave whole lifetimes proudly driving and servicing the engines, spending

Sunshine, steam and shadow play upon GWR 4–6–0 No. 6956 *Mottram Hall*, simmering in the old timber S&DJR shed at Bath Green Park. It was always a wonder that this building never went up in flames! The evening sun highlights the dilapidated state of both the shed and the locomotive. This sort of picture, sharp but with most of the detail hidden, can evoke much of the magic of steam – is the fiery beast alive? Great Western engines always looked wrong on S&D territory; this one bears the chalked shed code of 81F for Oxford.

(Revd Alan Newman, 28.8.65)

long hours in harsh conditions for modest reward. Cabs and sheds could be uncomfortably hot, cold and draughty, and the work was mostly dirty and physical. A suitable commemorative coat of arms for the ghosts of steam shedmen would be: argent, a steam locomotive with spanner and shovel honours, a chief of cotton waste and a navel of oil can, all sable, with supporters rampant of a driver dexter and fitter sinister, all proper, with the motto *Sie Dienten* (they served).

Another fascination of engine sheds was the seemingly infinite variety of layouts. Environment, topography, site area, connections and operational needs combined to make virtually every MPD unique. Layouts would also vary with time as operational needs grew (or declined) and as extensions were built upon adjacent land. The overall objective was to achieve a smooth flow of locomotives through all the various stages of arrival, servicing, storage and departure, avoiding, as far as possible, conflicting movements. Opinions were divided as to the optimum layout – roundhouse or straight shed, for example – or the best method of coaling. The 'shed' itself (storage under a roof) was but one element of the depot. Other elements included the turntable(s) and the yard sidings for ashing, watering, coaling, coal delivery, maintenance and unprotected storage.

The pictures in this chapter are taken mostly in front of the shed or by the coaler. They are portraits of steam which celebrate some 150 years of continuous development, with examples from the late nineteenth century to *c.* 1960 when development stopped. They were inherently inefficient machines, some 5–9 per cent thermal efficiency at best compared with some 18–25 per cent for diesels and electric cycles. With imperfect

operation, steam-raising, standing idle, blowing off, blowing down, leaks, spillages, etc., the annual efficiency of a steam engine fleet was just a few per cent (useful output divided by chemical energy of all the coal bought). Detailed design – from firebox to cylinders and exhaust – had approached the limits of perfection for that technology – coal grate, the shell boiler at 250 p.s.i., the reciprocating engine, and with few constraints on atmospheric emissions. Further developments might have been possible – fluidized beds with water-tubing, for example – but the beast would still have been inherently bulky, environmentally unfriendly, labour- and maintenance-intensive and operationally awkward (you cannot turn it on and off). The steam locomotive in the UK became outclassed for a whole series of reasons.

Some 20,000 steam locomotives entered BR service in 1948. BR built a further 999 of 'standard' design together with some hundreds of pre-nationalization design. Roger Bramley (*The Standard Steam Locomotives of British Railways*, David & Charles, 1984) quotes the number of classes entering BR service as 476. His breakdown (see bottom of page) is as follows, to which are added the standard classes of BR and those depicted in this book.

The number of classes is staggering, particularly of the LNER and the Southern. Our pictures are a fair representation of the steam locomotive population of the 1950s and 1960s, showing great contrasts in size, wheel arrangement and style. Every picture in the book is a small tribute to the steam engine, but this chapter puts particular emphasis upon the beast alone in its lair and in small prides. So study the form and enjoy the smoky atmosphere of the sheds and yards.

Railway of origin	LNER	LMS	GWR	SR	BR	Others
Total locomotives inherited by BR	6443	7844	4056	1807		
Total classes in BR service	206	110	73	87	12	
Total classes depicted herein	24	18	11	15	9	9

The Great Central MPD at Woodford Halse was exceptional for its huge size in a rural setting and its high standard of general cleanliness. The wide variety of motive power included J5 and J39 classes of 0–6–0, the J50 0–6–0 tank as well as C4 Atlantics, 'Black Fives' and 'Austerity' 2–8–0s. A surprise visitor from York was NER 4–6–0 class B16/3 No. 61421, seen here dropping ash. Beyond is 2–6–2 class V2 No. 60828, also from York. The V2s would be backed down to Banbury to take turns to Sheffield.

(Revd Alan Newman, 8.5.61)

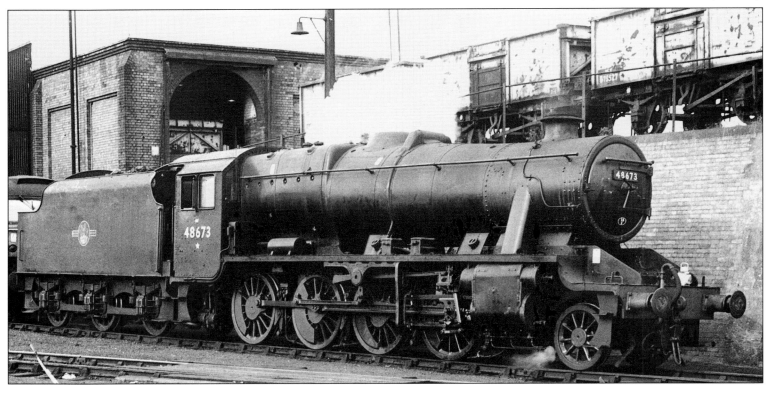

It was not always easy to portray the large, black LMS engines in a 'good light' when they were dirty, so this picture at Banbury MPD makes a pleasant change – even the yard is neat and tidy. Fresh from what was almost certainly its last works visit, Stanier 2–8–0 class 8F No. 48673 stands by the coaling plant, awaiting its next turn of duty. Although never 'beautiful', the design had a certain elongated elegance which spelt 'power and simplicity'. Introduced in 1935, there were 776 in the class and 6 are preserved.

(Eric Sawford, 27.10.65)

And now for something completely different: an 0–4–0 shunter which looks more like a van body than a steam engine. Manufactured at the Sentinel Wagon Works, class Y3 was introduced in 1925. Found mainly in the east of England, No. 68164 is pictured on a far outpost of the LNER in the shed yard of Wrexham Rhosddu. It is coaled up ready to work a short local mineral line. This west coast province of the Great Central was connected to the east via the Cheshire Lines system through Manchester.

(Maurice Dart, 26.8.52)

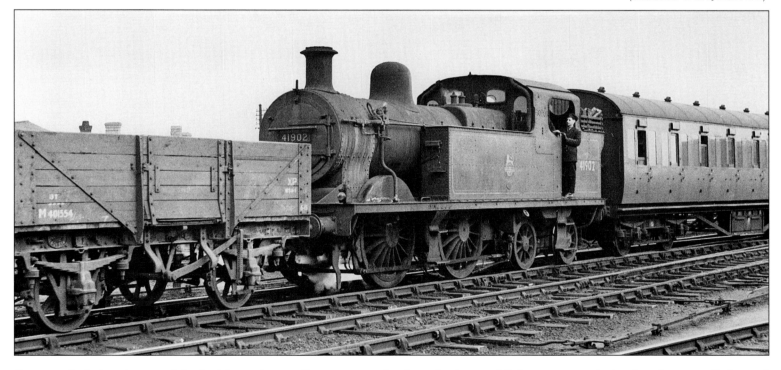

So many 0–4–4 tanks were inherited from the pre-Group companies for suburban and light passenger duties that there was little need for further new engines of this type. Sir William Stanier built just ten for the LMS, introduced in 1932 for push–pull working. At Bletchley, No. 41902 seems uncertain as to whether it is shunting goods or passenger stock. They were a handsome design. All were withdrawn by the late 1950s and none is preserved. The last survivor was based in Gloucester to work the Tewkesbury branch service.

(Eric Sawford, 29.4.56)

Stafford MPD was readily observed from the station platforms. It made a delightful spectacle, with a fan of some fifteen sidings and point levers. Standard class 5 No. 73025 is seen emerging beneath a cloud of its own steam, while another 4–6–0 makes smoke outside the shed. To the right, LMS 2–6–4 tank No. 42546 takes water by the great ferro-concrete 'Cenotaph' coaling

tower, while a pair of diesel shunters rest on a siding to the left. A final reminder of coal is the slender brick chimney of the platelayers' hut on the far left.

(Alan Postlethwaite, 18.8.62)

South Wales was a stronghold for many classes of 0–6–2 tank with origins on the pre-Grouping railways as well as the GWR. Looking excessively large for such a low BR number, ex-Rhymney Railway class R No. 38 stands on a sunny morning outside Cardiff, East Dock shed. Built in 1921 to the design of C.T. Hurry Riches for heavy freight traffic, its latter-day duties were mainly as shed pilot and trips up the Cardiff Railway route to Nantgarw. It was withdrawn and scrapped in October 1957.

(Maurice Dart, 21.4.57)

A challenge to the Great Western at Swansea was the LNWR, connected through Radnor and Brecknock from Shrewsbury and Crewe. Standing outside Victoria MPD at Swansea are a pair of 'Welsh rarebits', Webb 0-6-2 'Coal Tanks' Nos 58921 and 58880, a class which was introduced by the LNWR in 1881. They were probably better known by their LMS numbers 7782 and 27553. Although under the auspices of the Western Region, the Welsh LNWR sheds continued to house an interesting collection of LNWR stock including the large Beames 0–8–4 tanks.

(Revd Alan Newman, 23.7.53)

The Great Central Railway introduced 2–8–0 class O4 in 1911 for heavy freight duty. Many were built for the Railway Operating Division of the Royal Engineers for service in the First World War and 100 were subsequently acquired by the Great Western. Class ROD No. 3034 from Bristol St Philips Marsh shed is pictured at Radstock with a freight train on the North Somerset line.

(Revd Alan Newman, 7.2.53)

Yarmouth Beach shed, was the terminus of the M&GN line from Lynn, Peterborough and the Midlands. Class D16/3 No. 62524 was one of several rebuilt 'Clauds' on shed, accompanied by a selection of B12s and J17s. Introduced by the GER in 1900 to the design of James Holden, a total of 121 'Claud Hamiltons' were built, a most successful passenger 4–4–0 for that era.

(Eric Sawford, 18.8.57)

An 'atmospheric' scene in the yard of one of the East Coast main line sheds – Grantham – amid a forest of poles and with coal and ash littering the tracks. A relatively new 'Cenotaph' coaling tower in ferro-concrete contrasts with the more traditional ramp-type coaling stage found throughout Britain's railways. The prominent 'square' tender belongs to class A3 Pacific No. 60048

Doncaster, built at its namesake town in 1924. On the coaling line is class WD 2–8–0 No. 90032, built in Glasgow by the North British Locomotive Co. in 1943.

(Hugh Ballantyne, 3.8.63)

The 'Royal Scot' class 7P of 4–6–0, introduced by the LMS in 1927 to the design of the North British Locomotive Co., was rebuilt by BR with Stanier taper boilers. No. 46137 *The Prince of Wales' Volunteers South Lancashire* looks immaculate at Crewe North MPD with original high boiler and smoke deflectors. The LMS 'crimson lake' livery, however, has been replaced by BR lined black.

(Kenneth Oldham, March 1951)

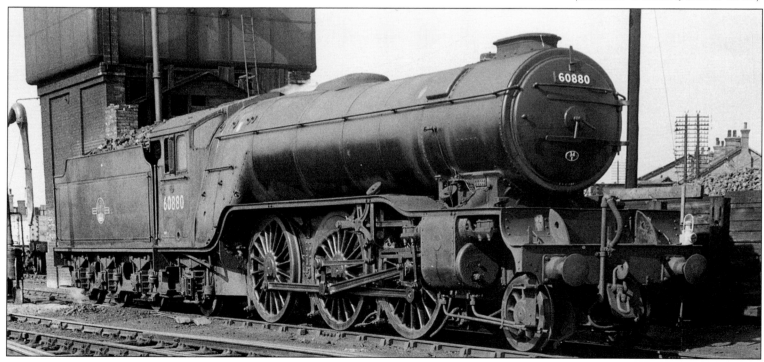

The elegant lines of LNER 2–6–2 class V2 are brought out in this shot of No. 60880 from New England depot, seen here on standby duty at Peterborough. The wheels and motion are enhanced by the gracefully shaped running plate. The firebox casing blends with the circumference of the huge boiler. The double chimney was a more recent addition.

(Eric Sawford, 6.9.62)

A study of two contrasting class 2 goods engines at Bescot MPD, Birmingham, nose-to-nose but generations apart by some seven decades! On the right is Ivatt Mogul No. 46457 of 1946 vintage of which 128 were built for mixed traffic. Centre, with a markedly lower running plate and boiler, is Johnson 0–6–0 goods engine No. 58185, one of the original batch of 120 built by the Midland Railway in 1875–6. Nearly 1,000 of these stalwarts were built and No. 58185 was one of the oldest steam engines still in BR service at that time.

(Revd Alan Newman, 26.4.62)

This ancient class of 0–6–0 general purpose locomotive was introduced by the Great Eastern Railway in 1883 to the design of T.W. Wordsell. Despite their small size, these powerful, sturdy engines provided sterling service for over seven decades on East Anglian freight and passenger services. Class J15 No. 65420 is an 'unfitted' example, seen here at Huntingdon.

(Eric Sawford, 14.6.56)

By mid-1962, BR was well into its programme of scrapping steam locomotives, and a visit to Darlington North Road yard showed that it was not just the older engines that were going. Barely twenty years of age, LNER 4–6–0 class B1 No. 61077 has already lost its boiler and motion and probably disappeared completely within a couple of days. Although sad and dishevelled, the frame, wheels and empty cab are still evocative. It is worth comparing with No. 61197 in prime condition (see p. 23).

(Brian J. Dickson, 27.7.62)

Locomotives under repair always make interesting subjects. LNER 0–6–0 class J38 No. 65910 is seen at Thornton MPD (by the Dunfermline–Dundee main line) with the middle set of driving wheels removed. Introduced by Gresley in 1926 for Fife coal traffic, all thirty-five of the class were still based in Scotland during the 1950s. They were a variation of the more numerous class J39 but with a longer boiler and smaller driving wheels. The 0–6–0 tank locomotive beyond is class J83 No. 68451, dating from 1900.

(Eric Sawford, 23.8.55)

The D49/1 was a handsome class of 4–4–0 light passenger engine which was introduced by the LNER in 1927 to the design of Sir Nigel Gresley. The first batch of thirty-six were named after shires served by the LNER, while a second batch of forty were named after hunts. They were all allocated to MPDs in the NE and Scotland. Alongside the 'straight' shed at Scarborough, No. 62723 *Nottinghamshire* is a visitor from Selby shed. On the road beyond is 2–6–2 class V2 No. 60941 from York shed.

(Maurice Dart, 19.8.60)

Hither Green was an entirely new MPD which opened in 1933 to serve the adjacent marshalling yard. The SR-style corrugated coal stage seen here had an engine road on either side leading to the turntable. Engine allocations were mainly for freight, including class W 2–6–4 tank No. 31912, seen here taking water. This class was a Maunsell development of the three-cylinder 2–6–0 class N1, and only fifteen were built for cross-London heavy freight transfers. None is preserved, but they were a familiar sight at Hither Green during the 1950s.

(Eric Sawford, 24.5.56)

The 9F was the heaviest and most numerous class of standard steam engine built by BR. Introduced in 1954 for heavy mineral traffic, a total of 251 were produced. For a short period when newly constructed, a batch of these 2–10–0s was allocated to the Southern Region shed at Eastleigh. From this batch, No. 92205 stands in winter sunlight alongside Westbury shed, resting between duties. Sister locomotive No. 92220 *Evening Star* was the final steam engine made for BR, turned out from Swindon works in 1960.

(Maurice Dart, 18.3.62)

The only significant challenge to the Great Western's monopoly of Bristol was the long Midland/LMS line from Birmingham, Gloucester and Bath. Bristol Barrow Road was a typical red-brick Midland roundhouse whose 'atmosphere' is captured here. There was never any difficulty in finding the place – you simply looked for the permanent pall of smoke by the gasholder! The locomotives are Ivatt 2–6–2 tanks Nos 41207 and 41304, and GW Pannier tank No. 9623. Who knows what lurks within the murk beyond.

(Revd Alan Newman, spring 1963)

A congregation of large engines at Crewe South MPD, all in sad condition during their latter days. There were no fewer than 93 locomotives on shed, the vast majority of which were 'Black Fives', standard 2–8–0s, 2–10–0s and one 'Britannia' (minus name-plates). The 'Black Five' in the centre is No. 44659. Note the dip in the track beneath its tender.

(Revd Alan Newman, 8.6.66)

Between 1936 and 1949, twenty-three LSWR 0–4–4 class O2 tanks were transferred to the Isle of Wight. They were modified for island working by the fitting of Westinghouse air brakes, enlarged bunkers and independent numbering. Inside the engine shed at Ryde St John's Road are No. 16 *Ventnor* (left) and, being prepared for service, No. 22 *Brading*. The roof trusses are

hand-me-downs from the LBSCR overhead ac electrification system which was replaced with the 'outside third' dc system during the early years of the SR.

(Revd Alan Newman, 9.9.64)

LMS class 4MT, introduced in 1947 by H.G. Ivatt was the basis of BR's standard class 4 Mogul. Respectively, 162 and 115 were built. Fresh from general overhaul, No. 43068 is seen here at Lincoln MPD on its way back to its home depot of South Lynn. Note the high running plate and high cab side, and the tablet exchange apparatus on the tender for working over the M&GN lines.

(Eric Sawford, 25.8.57)

SECR Class N Mogul No. 31853 is seen here at Hither Green shed, with a great water tank and coaling tower beyond. The class, introduced in 1917 to the design of Richard Maunsell, owed much to the GWR. Moguls (2–6–0s) were introduced to Britain *c.* 1900; GWR imported a batch of eighty from the USA. They were subsequently developed throughout the UK for mixed traffic duties.

(Eric Sawford, 24.5.56)

LNER class A4 Pacific No. 60004 *William Whitelaw* simmers quietly outside St Margaret's depot in Edinburgh. As Haymarket shed, on the western side of the city, became the main depot for diesel locomotives working out of Edinburgh, so St Margaret's became busier with the remaining steam engines. The grimy atmospherics evident here continued until April 1967 when the depot closed. The setting enhances rather than detracts from the beauty of Gresley's masterpiece. The locomotive is named after a chairman of both the LNER and the Forth Bridge Railway Company.

(Brian J. Dickson, 2.6.64)

81

A round-table conference at Bath Green Park by the turntable of the old Midland shed featuring 'Black Five' Nos 44945 (from Saltley) and 45252 (from Warrington) plus 0–6–0 class 4F No. 44571, also from Saltley. Considerable holiday traffic and pigeon specials meant that Bath saw an amazing variety of motive power during the summer months, including visitors from Crewe, Manchester, Liverpool and Sheffield, as well as Southern engines working up from Bournemouth.

(Revd Alan Newman, 23.7.55)

Sunderland MPD was one of the last strongholds of steam in the north-east. Its locomotive stud consisted mainly of the three types shown here (left to right): North Eastern Railway class J27, introduced in 1906 (0–6–0 No. 65855); NER class Q6, introduced in 1913 (0–8–0 No. 63437); and the Ministry of Supply class WD, introduced in 1943 (2–8–0 No. 90135). The J27s and Q6s were magnificent, going on to the end of steam. Although more plain and always filthy, the WDs also did sterling duty.

(Revd Alan Newman, 14.6.67)

VI

RAILWAY PEOPLE – THE OTHER MOTIVE POWER

Reversing the locomotive. Having an all-over roof and a tunnel approach, one of the few sunny spots at Liverpool Central was this corner for servicing. The crew is gently positioning LMS class 5 No. 45333 for watering, ashing and turning. This terminus (now closed) was once owned by the Cheshire Lines Committee, offering services to Warrington, Manchester and over the Peak District to Derby and St Pancras.

(Alan Postlethwaite, 27.8.60)

Like so many other industries of that era, the steam railway was manned on the principle of cheap labour working long hours until the age of sixty-five. With overtime, a working week of sixty hours or more was commonplace, incorporating nights, weekends and bank holidays for those on shift. The work could be arduous and dirty, and holidays were meagre – a few weeks at most. Railwaymen tended to develop a love-hate relationship with their work, especially at 4 a.m. on a cold winter's morning when they were roused from their beds by a cleaner from the shed. Though loving the nature of the industry, they could hate the strain and constraint that it imposed upon their lives. The ball-and-chain was accepted by most with a resigned cheerfulness.

Like other industries and the armed services, the steam railways were highly disciplined with a strict 'line-and-staff' hierarchy for management and promotion, a thick rulebook and penalties for non-conformity. The rewards were modest wages, camaraderie and a sense of a job well done (most of the time). On the footplate in particular, there was enormous pride, teamwork and a striving for perfection on every turn of duty. Such spirit and 'company loyalty' could also be found in industries such as mining, shipbuilding, iron and steel making, gas works, power stations and most manufacturing. But steam railways were different – special, one might say – for several reasons: the product moved from city to city thousands of times each day; railways were in intimate contact with their customers; and the steam railway was largely unautomated, i.e. it was out of date in the postwar era.

Being 'unautomated' meant that most trains were operated by hand, back and muscle (stoking, ashing, watering, valve operations, uncoupling, cleaning, etc.), points and signal levers were pulled manually, signal lamps had to be refilled with oil, level-crossing gates were pushed or hand-wheeled, general goods were mostly manhandled, track was maintained using hand tools and much labour,

records were kept in pen and ink, even the tickets had to be fetched by hand from the great racks. These were the issues that the Modernization Plan of 1955 sought to address and to reform. It succeeded, resulting in the halving of the workforce and the elimination of steam. However, much of the magic of railways was lost in the process. Those who worked and travelled during the last days of steam were witnessing a piece of social history coming to an end.

The pictures in this chapter concentrate upon those who worked on the lines, trains and stations, rather than those in central offices. Central clerks, planners, managers and specialists were rarely photographed, and yet it was they who controlled activities from day to day, year by year, and made the key decisions on investment, closures, timetables, marketing and working practices. Many a general manager rose from the ranks of the unseen clerks and planners, but none came from the train crews, signalmen, porters, fitters and engineers. Some station staff were promoted to the signal-box, the guards van or to central offices. A guard might rise to the rank of inspector.

A railway station would comprise offices for tickets, parcels and goods, served by porters, booking clerks, shunters, foremen and station master, with signalmen nearby. There were waiting rooms, toilets and sometimes a refreshment room, all of which had to serviced, cleaned and heated. Above every station was a forest of chimneys for coal fires, with a coal store 'round the back' or under the footbridge. Gas lights were individually lit; some stations still had oil lamps, while others had electric lighting. Platforms had to be swept, the edges re-whitened and the flower-beds tended. Overall, stations were alive with staff, bringing comfort and a sense of welcome to the traveller.

Life on the footplate started as a cleaner, a grade that encompassed filling, lighting, steam raising and putting engines to bed as well as internal and external cleaning and 'knocking-up' of crews. The cleaner was also a trainee fireman, the next grade up. Firemen started on the 'bottom link' – piloting and yard duties – and then progressed to freight trains, intermediate passenger trains and eventually expresses – the 'top link'. Firemen in turn were trainee drivers, but upon attaining that grade would restart on the 'bottom link' in yards, working their way up again. The top drivers were therefore much older men than their firemen, and most would hold their positions proudly until retirement at sixty-five, frequently achieving the magic fifty years of service and a gold watch.

In engine sheds and 'works', the career of a craftsman (or 'mechanic' as they were once called) was quite different. As in other engineering industries, he would serve an apprenticeship of some four to seven years and then be qualified for life. He might train as a general fitter or specialize as a boilermaker, turner, smith, or plater. His hours were more regular and mostly daytime, but the nature of the work could be variable. Workshops were often cold and draughty, and light repairs might have to be carried out on locomotives in yards or stranded elsewhere. He was supported by a 'mate' (labourer) and by the feedback of information from the train crews. His work was largely unseen by the general public and it was left to the railway enthusiast to seek him out.

With few exceptions, our pictures are taken in dry and mostly sunny weather, conditions that best suit the photographer–enthusiast. Little hint is given of the harsh realities of running and maintaining the system throughout the year, day and night. They depict an amiable body of people. Indeed, the people of the steam railway

Trimming the coal at Salisbury, generally the only stop for express services between Waterloo and Exeter. The crew was changed here, and all four would set about the tasks of filling the water tank and trimming the coal, aided by a cleaner (in white cap) from Salisbury shed. The cleaner was a jack of all manual tasks, on the first step to becoming a fireman and eventually a driver. Note the short-handled, long-faced stoking shovel leaning against the water column. The locomotive is an immaculate 'Merchant Navy' class Pacific No. 35014 *Nederland Line*.

(*Alan Postlethwaite, 3.7.62*)

were generally helpful and friendly to all. In rural areas in particular, there was usually time between trains to chat about the line and to reminisce about times past. Steam railway people were a proud breed and delighted in their industry.

Civil work is in progress at Bath Spa station, during the replacement of I.K. Brunel's skew bridge over the Avon. Construction workers stand aside to allow the slow passage, wrong-line working of the 10.10 (Sun) Cardiff to Portsmouth train, headed by GWR 4–6–0 No. 6932 *Burwarton Hall*. An engineers' train is on the Up line on the right, headed by a Collet 0–6–0 class

'2251'. The scene is intriguing. Many would instinctively want to join in the work, but it was not so attractive in foul weather or at night.

(Hugh Ballantyne, 25.10.59)

Holding the train at Port St Mary, Isle of Man. Semi-obscured in steam and smoke, a young family is busy on the platform, embarking or saying farewell, while the guard signals 'hold' to the driver of 2–4–0 tank No. 12 *Hutchinson*. This is the first station out of Port Erin, in a beautiful sylvan setting just a quarter of a mile from the sea. The island is full of historic railways; one can travel from end to end via the Manx Electric line from Ramsey, the Snaefell Mountain Railway, the Douglas horse tram and this quaint relic of steam.

(Alan Postlethwaite, 29.8.60)

Shunting in the Up bay at Stroud. It is not obvious who is the shunter, driver, fireman or porter. (Firemen acted as shunters where none was provided.) Other features of interest are the back of the Regal cinema, new lampposts, platform re-surfacing and Brunel's stone goods shed and offices. The locomotive is GWR Prairie tank No. 6128.

(Alan Postlethwaite, July 1964)

Oiling and greasing at Adelaide shed, Belfast. The crew attend to a driving wheel of class V No. 207 *Boyne* standing over an ash pit. At this time, only eleven 4–4–0s remained in service in the British Isles, all of GNR(I) origin and all at work on the UTA system. This engine, one of five delivered by Beyer Peacock in 1948, was later given high-sided tenders. They were a simple-expansion, 3-cylinder version of the pre-war Glover compounds; No. 85 is preserved at Whitehead, Co. Antrim.

(Hugh Ballantyne, 1.9.64)

Waiting passengers at Lockerbie are neatly graded, wearing light topcoats and spotted dresses. They are witnessing the arrival of LMS 'Jubilee' class 4–6–0 No. 45673 *Keppel* at the head of a London to Perth train. This 3-cylinder class was introduced by Sir William Stanier in 1934 for express passenger duty and 190 were built. At rest in the bay is Caledonian 0–4–4 tank No. 55234

sporting a most prominent stovepipe chimney; its full width, round-topped side-tanks are a legacy of LBSCR design brought north by Dugald Drummond.

(Ronald Toop, August 1959)

Going off-duty at Brighton shed. Despite being in a zone of 1930s electrification, the number and variety of steam locomotives allocated to Brighton was remarkable. R.J. Billington's final batch of 0–6–2 tanks was class E6, introduced in 1904 and represented here by No. 32418, retaining a characteristic Billington chimney. Other locomotives include a 'Terrier' 0–6–0 tank (left) and an Ivatt 2–6–2 tank (right).

(Revd Alan Newman, 5.8.62)

Open Day at Doncaster 'plant'. Young enthusiasts mingle with groups of fitters in the Crimpsall shop. Humans are dwarfed by the sheer scale of the shops with their overhead travelling cranes and line upon line of sad-looking, semi-dismantled engines. In the foreground is Peppercorn class A1 Pacific No. 60119 *Patrick Stirling* (see p. 3).

(Kenneth Oldham, April 1954)

Fitting in the yard at Eastleigh Works. Several groups of maintenance staff are working on Urie 4–6–2 tank class H16 No. 30518 from Feltham shed. This class of five engines was introduced in 1921 for heavy freight transfers across west London. They were latterly relegated to empty stock working out of Waterloo and for Fawley refinery traffic. Alongside, in pristine ex-works condition, is 'King Arthur' class N15 No. 30806 *Sir Galleron* from Hither Green shed. Both classes originated on the LSWR under the design supervision of Robert Urie.

(Maurice Dart, 4.9.58)

Platform services at Salisbury. An ice cream lady, a water man (for filling lavatory tanks), a selection of carts and barrows, and a porter carrying suitcases for a lady with a stick, witness the arrival of the west-bound 'Atlantic Coast Express', a smart train of Maunsell coaches headed by rebuilt SR 'Merchant Navy' class Pacific No. 35014 *Nederland Line*. The train announcement

is almost drowned by the roar of the safety-valve blowing. The raised signal beyond is for the imminent departure of a Westbury train.

(Alan Postlethwaite, 3.7.62)

Ashing out at Oxford MPD. When the 'Lord Nelson' class 4–6–0 was introduced in 1926, they were the pride of the Southern Railway, working crack expresses and kept in gleaming condition. In the latter days of steam, clean but not gleaming, No. 30855 *Robert Blake* takes a break, having handed over its train from the south. Beyond are Pannier tank No. 9455 and Prairie tank No. 4149. This visit was an observer's feast. Other engines included LMS 'Black Fives', an LNER K3 and a wide variety of GWR and BR types – the Big Four plus One!

(*Revd Alan Newman, 18.5.61*)

Opposite: Waiting for the bell in Dorrington signal-box on the Shrewsbury–Craven Arms line. Mr E.H. Marsh of Church Stretton is a model of perfect turnout. Reflecting the railway's emphasis on safety, he wears both belt and braces, and the box is immaculate. The bell, pushes and block instruments glimmer on the block-shelf. The rear catch handles and front-mounted function-plates are a common pattern for Britain and the GWR. The black and white chevrons are for a detonator lever. There was also a hand-generator here for a remote facing point (the limit of hand operation was 350 yards).

(*Alan Postlethwaite, 19.8.62*)

Closing the doors. 'A porter piles the parcels on the dray / the engine will uncouple and pull free / a family homeward wends its happy way / and leaves the train in sunshine and to me' (with apologies to Thomas Gray). The star of this pleasant summer scene is the porter, smartly turned out and attending to the luggage door of a GWR brake-composite. Another stationman has collected tickets and is returning to the main building. The locomotive is Ivatt Mogul No. 46509 and the location is Lanfyllin, terminus of a Cambrian Railways branch in mid-Wales.

(Alan Postlethwaite, 9.6.62)

Opposite: Setting the signal at Penkridge, the first signal-box out of Stafford on the Wolverhampton line, the site of a former LNWR station relegated to goods status. The goods shed and sidings can be seen through the age-distorted glass of the south window as Mr A. Hunt poses by his frame, rag in hand. Features include the track-diagram, telephone, two oil lamps, a tall desk with the train register, and a small tin of Nescafé on the stool. LNWR characteristics include loop-handles for the catch rods and a separate rear-board for the lever name-plates.

(Alan Postlethwaite, 8.8.62)

Water-filling at Basingstoke was a task for this top-link fireman, nicely balanced on the tender of a rebuilt Bulleid light Pacific. Earlier in the day, during coaling at Nine Elms, half a hundredweight of coal was spilled onto the vacuum cylinders and water tank but it was seldom the practice to shovel up such spillages. The fireman's job was arduous when one considers that his tasks had to be carried out in all weather conditions, at all seasons and times of day.

(Alan Postlethwaite, 11.6.63)

Sizing up the job. A stranger to Edinburgh, LMS class 8P Pacific No. 46256 *Sir William A. Stanier, FRS* has worked a special into the city and has reversed into St Margaret's depot for servicing. Having been coaled up and turned, two members of St Margaret's staff are contemplating the relative merits of this class against their usual LNER Pacific charges. On the other hand, they may just be admiring the sheer bulk of the locomotive. The 6 ft 9 in diameter driving wheels certainly make the men look diminutive.

(Brian J. Dickson, 29.3.64)

VII

SPECIAL TRAINS – SOME SURPRISE VISITORS

LNER class A4 Pacific No. 60031 *Golden Plover* departs the eastern end of Edinburgh Waverley on Easter Sunday with a Stephenson Locomotive Society special from Glasgow to Hawick and Carlisle. Entering service in 1937, *Golden Plover* spent most of its life allocated to Edinburgh's Haymarket shed. It was transferred to St Rollox in 1962 for the new Glasgow–Aberdeen 3-hour service until it was withdrawn and scrapped in 1965.

(David Hucknall, 18.10.65)

Trains are 'special' when they cannot be found in the published regular timetables. They include trains for troops, royals and enthusiasts, trains for track maintenance, inspection and weed-killing, test runs for locomotives leaving the works, and the locomotive exchange trials of 1948. They are generally one-offs, probably never to be repeated, providing pleasant surprises for those that encounter them – the icing on the cake.

About half the trains in this chapter are enthusiasts' specials, chartered by clubs and societies to run over unusual routes and/or with historic engines. Many were 'last opportunities' before lines, locomotive classes or steam in that area passed into history. Such 'railtours' and 'brake rides' were enormously popular during the 1950s and 1960s – indeed, they still are, but the choice is more limited. The pictures are a lasting tribute to the tolerance and enthusiasm of BR regional managements and to the imagination of the countless clubs and societies. Both parties had the vision to appreciate the significance of the end of steam.

The Railway Magazine and *Trains Illustrated* record a wealth of sponsoring societies. As well as stalwarts like the Railway Correspondence & Travel Society, the Stephenson Locomotive Society, the Locomotive Club of Great Britain and the Railway Enthusiasts Club, there were countless others of purely local membership or with specialist interests. Most of the embryonic preservation societies ran 'steam specials', as did railway clubs from the Universities of Oxford, Cambridge and London. 'Specials' were organized by many city and county societies of enthusiasts and modellers, as well as by the Railway & Canal Historical Society and the Narrow Gauge Railway Society; even the Westminster Bank had a society and who could ever forget the Society for the Reinvigoration of Unremunerative Branch Lines in the United Kingdom? All played their part in the enrichment and enjoyment of the last days of steam.

Nearly all the engines in this chapter were cleaned specially for the occasion and all are beautiful. However, David Hucknall's opening shot of *Golden Plover* stands out, not just because it is a fine and unusual side-composition but because of the unique, stunning styling of this class of locomotive, a masterpiece from Sir Nigel Gresley which deserves special mention. In a reworking of one of William Wordsworth's romantic poems,

My heart lifts up when I behold an A4 on the line;
So was it when I was a lad, so is it now I am a man,
So be it when I shall grow old – a sight so fine!

Instead of 'A4', you can substitute 'Princess', 'Castle', 'Arthur', 'Mogul' or any other two-syllable locomotive that is a personal favourite. (Note that in the poetic world, it is syllables not cylinders that count!) Whatever one's parochial favourite, the A4 stands out as the most distinctive and memorable of all the classes of UK steam engine. The flare of the running plate and the graceful curvature of the smokebox–boiler continuum cry out to studied and admired, whether viewed from the side (see p. 101), the front (p. 61) or from three-quarters on (pp. 16 and 81). The subtlety of the curves is such that the boiler appears to be humped above the leading and middle driving wheels, like the shoulders of a panther (although this is an illusion). The overall sleekness is enhanced by the lack of visible steam-pipes, putting great visual emphasis upon the double-chimney, protruding like the conning tower of a submarine.

The significance of the A4's streamlining was threefold: to reduce drag; to eliminate smoke-drift; and to promote good PR and prestige for the company. The 'drag factor' was important only at the highest speeds. In *The British Steam Locomotive, 1925–1965* (Ian Allan Ltd, 1966), O.S. Nock quotes a saving of 138 h.p. at 90 m.p.h. as a result of streamlining. Some 4–8 per cent of extra useful power was therefore available during a

The Exchange Trials of 1948 were an opportunity for some of the most powerful locomotives of the Big Four to be put through their paces in unfamiliar territory. Here at Doncaster, a Great Northern somersault signal gives the right of way for SR 'Merchant Navy' class Pacific No. 35019 *French Line CGT* on a preliminary run of the Leeds–King's Cross express. The Gresley coach confirms the LNER setting, its weathered teak contrasting with the immaculate malachite green of the engine. The black LMS tender was borrowed, since the Southern had no troughs or water pick-up appliances.

(Kenneth Oldham, May 1948)

typical long-distance journey. The 'PR factor' was evaluated not mathematically but as a managerial judgement, concluding that the prestige of possessing a world-beater in both appearance and speed, was priceless.

Study also some of the other fine locomotives in this chapter, mostly looking their best because they head special trains or are fresh from the works. Then imagine what the railways were like when all the engines were turned out virtually spotless for every turn of duty. If you need help, read some of C. Hamilton Ellis's vivid descriptions of colour, cleanliness and variety in the halcyon days of steam before the First World War. That was when every train was regarded as special.

During the early 1960s, the Gainsborough Model Railway Society arranged some imaginative railtours, including this trip to Aberystwyth and the Vale of Rheidol Railway. Here at Moat Lane, 4–6–0 No. 7800 *Torquay Manor*, first of the Great Western's 'Manor' class of 1938 vintage, takes water before starting its climb to Talerddig (283 ft in approximately 10 miles). The line started as the Newtown & Machynlleth Railway, one of the four original companies that amalgamated in 1864 to become the Cambrian Railways. Moat Lane station was closed on 31 December 1962.

(David Hucknall, 30.5.64)

Opposite: A 'steam special' with a difference, as a train of condemned Great Western 4–6–0s emerges from Stroud's Up goods yard to continue its funereal journey to a scrapyard further west. Four unidentified locomotives are headed by No. 6944 *Fledborough Hall*. Only the lead engine is in steam, the others having had their rods removed. All are in a filthy state, but the picture is given life by the brilliance of the lower-quadrant starting signals. GWR signals looked 'different', having slightly tapering arms which could be of different lengths according to function.

(Alan Postlethwaite, July 1964)

BR standard class 3 No. 77012 hurries along the MR line between Masborough and Chesterfield with what was noted as an 'Up troop train'. The photograph is taken by Canklow MPD in the Rother Valley. (Ickles Weir is hidden behind the timber-laden wagons.) The chimney and winding gear belong to Rotherham Main Colliery, now closed. No. 77012 is in good external condition, a credit to Farnley Junction shed, Leeds, where it was then housed.

(David Hucknall, 22.5.65)

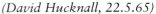

It is gratifying to the many clerical railway enthusiasts to have a class of engine honoured by the names of the saints of old. GWR 4–6–0 No. 2920 *Saint David* stands at Bath Spa, resplendent in lined black and red number-plate, fresh from overhaul at Swindon. This is the morning test run from Swindon to Bristol, leaving Bath at 8.45 and returning at about 11.15. The 'Saints' were the 2-cylinder outcome of Churchward's trials during the early 1900s between the 4–4–2 and 4–6–0 wheel arrangements.

(Revd Alan Newman, 14.9.51)

Great Eastern 0–6–2 tank class N7 No. 69614 has been beautifully cleaned to head the RCTS 'London and North Kent' railtour out of Liverpool Street. A stop on the North London line is at Canonbury where the engine is the centre of attention. Designed by A.J. Hill for suburban passenger service, a total of 134 were built between 1914 and 1927. Characteristics include the five-sided spectacles, round-topped windows and round-topped firebox. The enthusiasts show a wide range of clothing and ages but only one carries a camera. The platform debris looks like engine ash.

(Alan Postlethwaite, 21.3.59)

Swindon's ancient-looking wooden engine shed is the setting for a visitor from the LM region – 'Princess Coronation' class Pacific No. 46251 *City of Nottingham* – looking immaculate after working the outward leg of an RCTS special from Nottingham. Also on shed are two Great Western 4–6–0s, No. 7927 *Willington Hall* (smokebox door open) and No. 7022 *Hereford Castle* (left).

The latter was a standby for the Western Region/Ian Allan 'High Speed Castles Special' running from Paddington–Plymouth–Bristol–Paddington. Today *Willington Hall* is awaiting restoration by the Vale of Glamorgan Railway at Barry.

(Hugh Ballantyne, 9.5.64)

This RCTS special ran from Liverpool Street to East Finchley, then down to King's Cross and the 'Widened Lines' to the SECR. A class frequently used for this cross-London freight route was the GNR 0–6–0 tank class J50. Designed by Sir Nigel Gresley, a total of 102 were built between 1922 and 1937. This bow shot at Finsbury Park shows No. 68987 about to take up the running. Note the massive 1,520-gallon side-tanks with sloping fronts, and the semaphore signal reflected in the spectacle plate. The fluorescent lamps appear incongruous with the old GNR valanced canopies.

(Alan Postlethwaite, 21.3.59)

An LNWR stronghold in the Midlands was Bescot MPD, near Walsall. The original shed code of this important freight centre was 3B but in later years it changed to 21B, Saltley holding on to 21A. Several of those remarkable LNWR 0–8–0s had their home there. This class was introduced in 1912, commonly known as 'Super Ds'. The shed staff kindly positioned No. 48930 for this photograph; it had been cleaned up for an enthusiasts' special.

(Revd Alan Newman, 6.6.62)

The pioneer of standard gauge line preservation was the Bluebell Railway, opening in 1958 between Sheffield Park and Horsted Keynes. Until 1963, it was connected with BR here at Horsted Keynes. This 'Blue Bell' ran from Victoria, hauled by LBSCR class E4 No. 473 *Birch Grove* and a pilot. Built in 1898 to the design of Robert Billington, *Birch Grove* is the only survivor of its class, resplendent here in authentic umber livery.

(Eric Sawford, 31.3.63)

A lucky shot of the royal train passing High Dyke signal-box, headed by class A3 Pacific No. 60044 *Melton*. The Queen was travelling down the East Coast main line from Hitchin to Ballater to resume her holiday, having come up specially from Balmoral to attend the funeral of Sir David Bowes-Lyon. The brilliance of the train is achieved by means of an immaculately clean green locomotive, the royal train code of four lamps (a full set) and a marvellous collection of coaches in royal train maroon livery, some of them twelve-wheelers.

(Hugh Ballantyne, 16.9.61)

The evening sun glistens on the number-plate of Ivatt 2–6–0 class 2 MT No. 46506, as it heads an engineer's special train east of Cranmore on the GWR double-ended branch between Yatton and Witham. Paint is peeling from the fixed-distant signal, but it is securely bolted to its tapered wooden post. The branch was built as the East Somerset Railway, part of which is now preserved for steam, based at Cranmore West (the 'Strawberry Line'). Originally broad gauge with a terminus at Wells, it was later extended to join with the Bristol & Exeter's branch from Yatton.

(Alan Postlethwaite, 1.7.62)

VIII

PRESERVED FOR POSTERITY – A LEGACY OF STEAM

Following clearance trials in the previous month, the privately owned 4–6–0 No. 7029 *Clun Castle* overcomes a significant slip at the west end of Newcastle's platform 9 to haul a special towards King Edward VII bridge and the south. Built to GWR design, this BR locomotive entered service in 1950 and hauled the last steam train out of Paddington in 1965. It is preserved at the Birmingham Railway Museum, Tyseley.

(David Hucknall, September 1967)

As 'going concerns' to carry ordinary traffic throughout the year, steam railways in the UK ceased to exist in the late 1960s. What survived were essentially holiday lines or closed short lines in the process of being restored for steam by societies of volunteers. However, a large number of steam locomotives and associated rolling stock had been preserved or were being acquired, in some cases simply by 'earmarking' at the scrapyard. The situation is the same today except that the number of preserved lines and locomotives has escalated beyond all expectations and steam specials have been restored to run on specified sections of the main network. This chapter shows pictures from the 1960s of steam lines and locomotives which can be seen today in preserved form. So where did it all begin?

First are the narrow gauge steam railways which never closed (other than during war years). They survived the turbulent changes of the 1950s and 1960s by shedding their traditional local traffic to become holiday lines, funded mainly by tourists. Paramount among these is the Talyllyn Railway, the pioneer of all preservation societies which took over the old slate-carrying line as early as 1951, led by author and engineer, L.T.C. Rolt. The other remarkable Welsh mineral line to achieve continuity of operation is the Vale of Rheidol which remained

A test for Great Western engines and their crews was the Dainton bank between Newton Abbot and Totnes – the final section to the tunnel is at 1 in 37. Brunel fitted this section with the 'atmospheric' system of train propulsion but it was abandoned before use. GWR 4–6–0 No. 7027 *Thornbury Castle* makes an impressive sight on the final ascent, approaching the tunnel with the Down 'Royal Duchy' express, the 1.30 p.m. Paddington to Penzance. Today *Thornbury Castle* is being restored by the Waterman Railway Heritage Trust at 'The Railway Age', Crewe Heritage Centre.

(Hugh Ballantyne, 17.5.58)

under BR ownership until 'privatized' in 1989. Other narrow gauge lines to achieve continuity are the Snowdon Mountain Railway (rack and pinion) and three miniature (15-in) railways – the Fairbourne, the Ravenglass & Eskdale and the Romney, Hythe & Dymchurch.

Next are the narrow gauge lines without continuity of operation, which were once closed as uneconomic or unfit for their traditional traffic. The Isle of Man line from Douglas to Port Erin closed for just one season (1966) before being rescued for tourism by the island's government. The Ffestiniog is perhaps the most remarkable of them all. Having closed in 1946, it re-opened in stages from 1954 to 1982 through 13½ miles of rugged mountain terrain. The Welshpool & Llanfair is also well loved and more pastoral; it closed in 1956 and re-opened between 1964 and 1980.

The greatest collection of standard gauge steam locomotives, rolling stock and associated relics belongs to the National Railway Museum based at York. It is 'great' not simply for its size (some eighty steam locomotives) but because it comprises a fair representation of British types and affiliations. Established by Statute in 1968, the Museum opened in 1975. Older items were inherited from the Big Four and the BTC Museum of British Transport at Clapham. Some locomotives are kept available for loan on preserved lines and for steam specials.

There are many smaller locally flavoured museums in England, Scotland, Wales and Northern Ireland for the storage, restoration and static display of steam locomotives, carriages, etc. Next are the 'steam centres' which operate locomotives and brake vans on short sections of track at weekends and holidays. Then we come to the big steam centres – sites of old engine sheds – where steam locomotives are based, overhauled and prepared for heavy-duty steam specials on BR lines.

Finally we have the preserved standard gauge lines which vary in length from a mile or so to as much as 16 miles (Severn Valley Railway) and 20 miles (West Somerset Railway). They rely for success upon volunteer labour, kindly investors, seasonal tourism, visiting enthusiasts, local goodwill and the occasional 'windfall'. Rolling stock restoration societies frequently inhabit corners of the station sites, often taking a decade or more to restore a single engine. There are scores of such railways, some still in their infancy. The pioneer was the Bluebell Railway which started operation before the end of BR steam and is today striving to re-open the final section of its 10½-mile line through the Sussex Weald to East Grinstead.

Our pictures show a dozen engines from the last days of steam, representing some 450 that have been preserved in the UK. Their bases are identified but are liable to vary from year to year because of loans and transfers. Exactly which are serviceable also varies as boiler certificates expire and overhauls become due. What stands out from this modest collection is the variety of types, from the tiny 0–4–0 tank to the mighty Pacifics. So judge which are the most pleasing. The message is that at modest cost you can still experience the thrill of steam and something of the way of life that went with it. After riding the line, have a look in the cab, talk to the crew, or take a course to learn to drive one! It works wonders for the soul to dwell awhile in the steamy past. Enjoy your trips!

Peppercorn class A2 'Pacific' No. 60532 *Blue Peter* prepares to leave Newcastle Central with an Up King's Cross express. Built in 1948, this was the first of its class to emerge as new with a full BR number on the cab and 'British Railways' on the tender. The standard LNER apple-green livery was retained, however, making this a rare picture, since it was repainted in BR dark green in September 1949, acquiring a double chimney and a number on the smokebox door at the same time. Restored to apple green, it is now preserved by the North Eastern Locomotive Preservation Group for main line running.

(Kenneth Oldham, July 1948)

On the North Staffordshire Railway main line near Trentham, LMS class 5MT No. 44871 heads a coal train southwards, probably bound for Meaford or another power station. This locomotive was built in 1945 and has been preserved by a private owner and given the name *Sovereign*. It is normally kept and overhauled at Bo'ness, on the preserved steam line west of Edinburgh. It is one of an élite group of engines still used for main line running, and for this purpose it was stabled for some time at Steamtown, Carnforth (north of Lancaster).

(Alan Postlethwaite, 17.3.62)

LSWR 0–4–0 tanks on parade at Eastleigh Works. 'Sitting ducks' for the camera are class C14 No. 30589 and class B4 Nos 30096 and 30082. The latter appear to be ex-works in plain black while the former has been graced with lining-out. The B4s were introduced by Adams in 1891 for docks shunting, and No. 30096 is preserved on the Bluebell Railway. The C14 dates from 1906, designed by Drummond as a 2–2–0 for motor-train working but rebuilt by Urie for use as a shed pilot. To the right is 4–6–0 class S15 No. 30827.

(Revd Alan Newman, 24.6.54)

With rain lashing down, the crew kept well inside the cab of Sligo, Leitrim & Northern Counties 0–6–4 tank class Z No. 27 *Lough Erne*, shunting in the yard at Belfast York Road. This locomotive and its sister No. 26 *Lough Melvin* were built by Beyer Peacock and delivered in 1950–1. Following closure of the SL&NCR in 1957, they became UTA stock in 1959, confined to shunting at York Road. The yard closed in the mid-1960s but *Lough Erne* is preserved by the Railway Preservation Society of Ireland at the Whitehead Excursion Station, Co. Antrim.

(Maurice Dart, 22.4.65)

A sylvan setting for a five-coacher headed by 2–4–0 tank No. 12 *Hutchinson* at Port St Mary, en route to Douglas. The old wooden coaches, of varied design and height, have fine panelling and twin running-boards, reminiscent of many Victorian trains on the mainland. This line to Port Erin is the only survivor of the financial crisis of the late 1960s and early 1970s. After closure

for one season, it was rescued by the IOM Tourist Board, the Marquis of Ailsa and the Tynwald. *Hutchinson* remains one of the serviceable locomotives.

(Alan Postlethwaite, 29.8.60)

A.H. Peppercorn's 2-cylinder class K1 Mogul was of LNER lineage. It was introduced in 1949 and seventy-one were built. They were still much in evidence in the north-east during the latter days of steam, most of them shedded at Sunderland, Middlesbrough and Tyne Dock, usually in a somewhat grubby condition. No. 62005 is exceptionally clean at Tyne Dock MPD, pulled out specially for the camera, having been spruced up for a royal occasion. It is preserved by the North Eastern Locomotive Preservation Group, and is frequently seen on the North Yorkshire Moors Railway at Pickering.

(Revd Alan Newman, 14.6.67)

The Lakeside branch of the Furness Railway was opened in 1869 to connect with steamers at a purpose-built quay at the south end of Lake Windermere. Following the Leven valley, it was 7½ miles long and made a triangular junction with the Furness 'main line' at the north end of Morecambe Bay. With passenger services only in the summer, LMS 2–6–4 class 4 tank No. 42589 is photographed departing Lakeside with a train to Ulverston. Two members of this class are preserved on a 3½-mile section of the branch, running between Lakeside and Haverthwaite.

(Ronald Toop, August 1959)

Clear lettering says it all on the locomotive and 20-ton private-owner coal wagons. The CEGB's 0–6–0 tank MEA No. 1 was built in 1951 by Robert Stephenson & Hawthorn Ltd to serve the extensive coal sidings and tipplers of Meaford power station, located in the Trent Valley between Stone and Stoke. This engine is preserved by the North Tynedale Steam Railway, based at North Shields. The scene has historical interest since both the power station and the CEGB are now defunct – only the locomotive has survived.

(Alan Postlethwaite, 13.3.62)

Lancashire was the last outpost of BR standard gauge steam which ceased on 11 August 1968. Just four months before the end, LMS class 5 No. 45025 approaches Salwick on the Fylde Coast line, with a Blackpool to Manchester Redbank parcels train. This locomotive was built in 1934 and is preserved by the Watkinson Trust on the Strathspey Railway, a Highland line which connects Aviemore with Boat of Garten, famous for its ospreys.

(Hugh Ballantyne, 10.4.68)

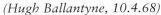

Ivatt Atlantic class C1 No. 251 was built by the Great Northern Railway in 1902 and is preserved at the National Railway Museum, York. After restoration to GNR livery, it is seen here at Marple double-heading the 'Northern Rubber Special', an annual outing to Blackpool organized by steam locomotive preservationist, Alan Pegler. The second engine is 4–4–0 'Director' class D11 No. 62663 *Prince Albert*, an early member of a class introduced in 1919 by the Great Central Railway.

(Kenneth Oldham, late summer, 1954)